MAYA

The Riddle and Rediscovery
of a Lost Civilization

Bonampak, Chiapas

MAYA

The Riddle and Rediscovery
of a Lost Civilization

by

CHARLES GALLENKAMP

Drawings by **JOHN SKOLLE**

DAVID McKAY COMPANY, INC.
New York

Foreword

DURING the first millennium of the Christian Era—while the Goths and Vandals overran central Europe, Mohammed united the Arabic tribes, and Charlemagne revived the Holy Roman Empire—men of a different genre were nurturing civilizations to maturity in the New World. Neither half of the earth's peoples then suspected the other's existence: the hemispheres of east and west were separated by uncharted oceans and thousands of years.

Scattered across the vast wilderness of "Middle America"—southern Mexico, the Yucatán Peninsula, and the Guatemalan-Honduran highlands—are inestimable numbers of monuments left behind by the progenitors of the most advanced civilization ever to evolve in Indian America—that of a people called the Maya. It is with the discovery and elucidation of these remnants of forgotten splendors that this book is concerned.

As a science, Mayan archaeology is scarcely a hundred years old. For almost four centuries following the conquest by Spain of the territories of Middle America the ruined cities that stood as mute testimony of the prowess of Mayan culture remained in obscurity. Only since the last half of the nineteenth century have scholars seriously labored to resurrect the startling accomplishments of the Maya from the earth. It was soon discovered that they were facing problems of multiple complexity within a geographical area of immense proportions and difficult terrain.

Any attempt to reconstruct Mayan history in its entirety would be presumptive; innumerable facets of research remain to be satisfactorily resolved, and much that is already known may yet have to be revised in the light of succeeding discoveries.

One of the fascinating aspects of archaeology is that it concerns not only the piecing together of events long since past in the erratic progression of human history, but that it enables us to trace the progress of ideas and institutions to the present day, and provides a measure by which to gauge the possible course of future history. As with any scientific study, certain purely technical data must be reduced to understandable terms in order to bring its broader significance into focus. It is this "practical" value of archaeology—its revelation of the successes and failures of long vanished civilizations—that affords its importance as a science. The knowledge brought to light by excavations in the Classical Lands and Asia Minor has proved invaluable to a better understanding of the era in which we live. Indeed, the very foundations of Western Civilization are traced to those areas which at first seem remote to the present day. Yet buried there was much that bore profoundly upon our times. So it may ultimately be with the prehistory of the New World; and the flowering of Mayan culture represents the most eloquent expression of civilized attainments known in ancient America.

The author wishes to express his gratitude to the following persons and institutions whose cooperation made possible the preparation of this manuscript: Dr. Ignacio Bernal, Director, Monumentos Prehispanicos, Mexico City; Dr. Luis Aveleyra Arroyo de Anda, Director, Museo Nacional de Antropología, Mexico City; Dr. Eusebio Davalos Hurtado, Director, Instituto Nacional de Antropología e Historia, Mexico City; Dr. Carlos Samayoa Ch., Director, Instituto Nacional de

Antropología e Historia, Guatemala City; Antonio Tejeda F., Director, Museo Nacional, Guatemala City; Robert E. Smith and the staff of the Carnegie Institution of Washington for helpful guidance in Yucatán and in the location of research material; Mr. and Mrs. John Clayton Jacobs, Jr., of Houston, Texas, for the use of their extensive library; my friend John Skolle for his invaluable assistance in the field and his lucid illustrations; Tony Bamford for her devoted efforts in preparing the final manuscript.

A special note of appreciation is extended to the Instituto Interamericano in Denton, Texas, and its director, Carl B. Compton, for the generous and continuing cooperation afforded me in planning and conducting the series of expeditions during which much of the contents of this book, photographic and otherwise, were collected.

CHARLES GALLENKAMP

Santa Fe, New Mexico

Preface

FOR more than a hundred years archaeologists and travelers have been fascinated by the enormous ruins which comprise the material remains of one of the high civilizations of the world—the Maya. When Caesar was subduing the barbarous tribes in what is now the greater part of Continental Europe, a vast complex of ceremonial cities was beginning to rise proudly in colorful splendor in the tropical regions of Middle America. When Richard I of England set off on the third Crusade against the infidel, the rich and complicated civilization of lowland Middle America had almost run its course. By the time the great revival of Humanism known as the Renaissance had fully begun—a movement which indirectly was to doom all of the indigenous civilizations of the Americas—the last great culture of Middle America had arisen in Tenochtitlán. The fabric of indigenous culture, including the Maya, was caught up by two great militaristic groups—the Aztec and the Inca—who were themselves soon to fall before the onslaught of conquerors from a far and alien land.

It is of the rise and decline of the Maya that the author of this book speaks. This is a book intended primarily for the general reader; its format is purposefully not that of a work designed solely for the professional archaeologists. Much has been written of the Maya; by and large this has been either rather technical archaeological writing or it has been journalism. The former is usually too specialized or tedious for the ordinary reader; the latter too often sacrifices truth for romantic effect.

In this volume the author has striven to avoid the complications of most books dealing with pre-Columbian cultures. Rather than detail in all their complexities the many sites and centers of Mayan life and ceremony, he has selected those sites and those elements which, when combined, give a readable and delightful account of the rise of Maya civilization and its inexorable march through pride and glory to extinction. It is the purpose here to present an accurate and truthful account in terms which the ordinary reader can understand and enjoy.

Though the author has visited and photographed virtually all of the important Maya sites on various occasions, this book is not presented as the result of his personal field work. Rather, he has examined the work of the scholars in the Mayan field and has presented a synthesis oriented to a central pattern. He has tried, in most cases, to begin with a specific problem and trace its solution as far as evidence permits. Where there are points of controversy among scholars, and there are several rather hotly contested ones, he has presented the several viewpoints. This volume is, of course, by no means the last word on the Maya nor does it purport to be anything of the sort. It is an excellent summary of what we know thus far of a mysterious, brilliant, and fascinating civilization.

CARL B. COMPTON
Instituto Interamericano
Denton, Texas

Grateful acknowledgments are made to the following for permission to quote from their publications:

Archaeology and Alberto Ruz Lhuillier: "The Mystery of the Temple of the Inscriptions"; Carnegie Institution of Washington: *Bonampak, Chiapas, Mexico,* by K. Rupert, J. E. S. Thompson, and T. Proskouriakoff; Denver Museum of Natural History: *Ancient Man in North America,* by H. M. Wormington; Farrar, Straus and Cudahy, Inc., and Routledge & Kegan Paul, Ltd.: *The Discovery and Conquest of Mexico,* by Bernal Díaz del Castillo, translated by A. P. Maudslay; Harper & Brothers: *The Antediluvian World,* by Ignatius Donnelly; Houghton Mifflin Company: *People of the Serpent,* by E. H. Thompson; M. Wells Jakeman: *The Origins and History of the Mayas;* New York Graphic Society: *Mexico, Pre-Hispanic Paintings;* Peabody Museum, Harvard University: *Relacíon de las cosas de Yucatán,* by Diego de Landa, translated by Alfred M. Tozzer; Rutgers University Press: *Incidents of Travel in Central America, Chiapas, and Yucatán,* by John L. Stephens; *The Saturday Evening Post,* Alberto Ruz Lhuillier, and J. Alden Mason: "The Mystery of the Mayan Temple"; School of American Research and Museum of New Mexico: *Florentine Codex, General History of the Things of New Spain,* by Fray Bernardino de Sahagún, Arthur J. O. Anderson and Charles E. Dibble, translators and editors; Charles Scribner's Sons: *The Temple of the Warriors,* by Earl H. Morris; Stanford University Press: *The Ancient Maya,* by Sylvanus G. Morley; University Museum: *The American Collections of the University Museum: The Ancient Civilizations of Middle America,* by J. Alden Mason.

Contents

Illustrations

MAYA

The Riddle and Rediscovery
of a Lost Civilization

CHAPTER 1

Discovery and Conquest

ON the morning of March 3, 1517, an Indian sentry guarding an outpost on the northern coast of Yucatán saw three dark objects interrupt the distant horizon. As they drifted nearer the shore he discerned that they were like mountains risen out of the sea on clouds. He went at once to summon his chieftain and the townspeople to have them witness their approach.

On board the sailing vessels bearded men with reddened, weary eyes rejoiced at the sight of land after riding out the fury of a tropical storm. Its winds had driven them far off their intended course—a slave-hunting expedition to the newly discovered islands of Guanajes, which lay between Cuba and Honduras. They had sailed from the port of Axaruco by commission of Diego Velásquez, the governor of Cuba, and were commanded by a respected hidalgo named Hernández de Córdoba.

Eagerly the seamen lined the rails of their ships as the unfamiliar coast line took form out of the white morning haze. Soon they were able to distinguish the rock-strewn beach which melted into a far-reaching savannah unbroken either by mountains or forests. The land was unknown to them. It was without a name, and existing charts failed to record its presence in these waters.

An astonishing sight was visible in the distance: rising up as though an outgrowth of the native limestone was a high wall enclosing a series of terraced pyramids and palace-like

3

buildings constructed of carefully fitted stones. Was this a delirious aftermath of their exhaustion? A magnificent walled city on a barren New World coast where only half-naked "savages" had ever before been encountered!

The two smallest caravels proceeded closer to shore in search of a safe anchorage, and the apparition could no longer be questioned. Before them was the splendid stone city "standing two leagues back from the coast." At a distance its structures rose up like the minarets of Islam and the Spaniards called it Great Cairo.

As the following day dawned upon the placid sea, a curious procession formed on the beach and set out toward the ships—ten longboats manned by as many as forty Indians apiece. Under a palm-thatch canopy at the rear of the largest vessel sat a retinue of chieftains accompanied by warriors armed with spears and shields. As they drew nearer, Córdoba extended gestures of friendship which were acknowledged by the natives, and minutes later they climbed aboard the flagship.

They were handsomely dressed in cotton shirts and breechclouts. Their manner was assured and they spoke a language wholly unfamiliar to the Spanish, who sought to convey their interest in the newly discovered land by means of signs. But the Indians soon indicated their wish to depart and were presented with strings of glass beads by their hosts.

The next morning they reappeared, bringing with them a number of empty boats. The chiefs beckoned the Spaniards to accompany them ashore. Córdoba's curiosity was sufficient to quell the reticence of his better judgment. He ordered his own longboats lowered; his seamen, armed with crossbows and muskets, crowded aboard them and started ashore behind the swiftly moving native craft.

Ahead of them the beach was lined with Indians who had come out from the city to view the curious strangers. Encouraged by their peaceful reception, the Spaniards followed the entourage of chieftains inland through an area of brush-covered hillocks. Suddenly loud shrieks filled the air, and warriors lying in waiting behind the mounds began to shower volleys of arrows down upon the terrified foreigners, leaving fifteen wounded after the first onslaught. Seeing that their enemy was taken by surprise, hoards of yelling natives darted from their hiding places and plunged into their disorganized ranks. They were awesomely arrayed in feather-crested helmets, knee-length cotton armor, and carried brightly painted shields, spears, and slings.

By then the Spanish had flung themselves behind mounds and rocks and brought their muskets into play. Sporadic thunderings roared out amid spurts of white smoke. Numbers of the oncoming Indians fell before the startled eyes of their allies who had never witnessed death so violent or so swift. Were they demons—these chalk-white men who rode upon the sea in floating mountains and whose smoking sticks spread sudden death? And the warriors hurled the last of their lances and fled in terror.

For the moment the superiority of their weapons had saved Córdoba's force from destruction. A renewed attack was certain to come; yet once within sight of the mysterious pagan city from whose ornate buildings great sculptured heads of serpents, jaguars, and demon-like creatures looked out across the faceless jungle, the Spaniards could not resist the lure of venturing farther. Ahead they came to a small plaza enclosed by three temples constructed of stone with thatched roofs. The buildings had been deserted minutes before, and the pungent odor of incense still hovered inside them.

Entering their narrow doorways, the conquistadors were aghast at the sight that befell them: here was a vision of barbaric splendor never conceived in their wildest illusions of pagan kingdoms. Nor had discoveries elsewhere in the territories of New Spain hinted at the existence of anything so

grand. Along the back walls of the temples stood altars of
stone with curious figurations deeply carved in their surfaces.
Some were of richly costumed chieftains or priests seated upon
thrones, others appeared to be human heads joined to animal
or serpentine bodies like weirdly distorted centaurs. Elsewhere
were entwined serpents with the heads of dragons, and rows
of unintelligible inscriptions which, even had they troubled,
the Spaniards could not have read—they were like no other
known writings.

Resting on the altars were images and idols molded of pottery, "some with the faces of demons or women and other
evil figures. . . ." Wooden chests overflowed with figurines in
the shapes of animals and birds, fashioned of copper and low-
grade *gold!*

However inferior the quality of the gold might have been,
Spanish avarice had been set aflame. Hastily the objects were
collected and carried to their waiting ships. Córdoba was determined to explore more of this land that now promised the
rewards which a generation of his countrymen had traveled to
the ends of the earth to seek. Steering seaward, they departed
without regret from the place which they called "Cape
Catoche."

For the Spanish the advance toward the New World was
impelled by dreams of finding a legendary El Dorado. The
flaming vision of undiscovered kingdoms, of mysterious lands
"where the sands sparkled with gems, and golden pebbles as
large as birds' eggs were dragged in nets out of the rivers," had
lured adventurers from Castile onto the unknown Western Sea.

In vain they had searched for the manifestations of their
glorious illusion: the golden Temple of Doboyda, the Fountain
of Eternal Youth, the jeweled sepulchers of Zenu, and the elusive passage to Cathay and the Spice Islands. But of undisclosed kingdoms they were to know much more than their
previous apparitions revealed.

The path of discovery had brought them to a land of track-less jungles scarred by volcanic mountains out of which arose resplendent cities of stone. Driven by the petulant spirit of conquest, eager for wealth and the royal favor to be gained by planting the banner of their sovereign at the gates of unclaimed frontiers, the Spaniards looked to these new shores with avid interest. They were unaware that their quest was soon to plunge them into the heart of the Mayan empire and a death struggle with the defenders of the most brilliant civilization ever to burst upon the darkly obscured horizon of American prehistory.

Unknowingly, Hernández de Córdoba had presaged this turning point in history. On the sands of Cape Catoche the disciples of opposite worlds had at last been hurled together in the clash of arms. Each represented amply the destiny be-fallen to their separate heritage: after a thousand years of florescence—during which a singularly accomplished civilization had risen out of the illimitable jungles of an unknown continent—Mayan fortunes were disastrously eroded by decline. Inversely, the Spanish domain, vigorous and expanding, had seized the helm of leadership in the Western world. Its seamen had been the knights-errant of the Age of Exploration which now stirred the nations of Europe; its royal coffers overflowed with wealth, and its armed might was so far invincible.

The Spanish consciousness of the sixteenth century was perfectly suited to the lures of discovery and conquest. The fearful mysteries of the seas had been abolished by the early voyages of Columbus—a challenging world lay beyond! In *The Conquest of Mexico* William Prescott wrote of the temptations now beckoning the restless Spaniards: ". . . the fascinations of a desperate hazard, on which the adventurer staked all his hopes of fortune, fame, and life itself. It was not often, indeed, that he won the rich prize which he most coveted; but then he was sure to win the meed of glory, scarcely less dear to his chivalrous spirit, and, if he survived to return to his home, he had wonderful stories to recount of perilous chances among the strange people he had visited, and the burning climes, whose rank fertility and magnificence of vegetation so far surpassed anything he had witnessed. . . . These reports added fresh fuel to imaginations already warmed by the study of those tales of chivalry which formed the favorite reading of the Spaniards. . . . Thus romance and reality reacted on each other, and the soul of the Spaniard was exalted to that pitch of enthusiasm which enabled him to encounter the terrible trials that lay in the path of the discoverer."

But the sons of Spanish soil shared a dualistic dream: to spread by any feasible method the tenets of their holy faith while growing rich on the spoils of conquest. And their parallel aspirations necessitated all manner of duplicity: lust for gold wore the mask of piety, fanatic personal ambition was heralded as devotion to a national cause, cruelty became the means by which heathens were reclaimed into the family of mankind, enslavement was made their hope of salvation. Against the nations of the American Indian was once again to be pitted the monstrous oppression of overgrown regimes and dogma.

What hideous apparitions were in store for Indian eyes to behold! Out of the foaming sea, like alien gods, there would soon emerge waves of white-skinned men of war encased in suits of metal. Some would ride upon the backs of four-legged creatures as though horse and man were detachable parts of the same unearthly monster. With them would come their smoking sticks and even more terrible instruments of destruction with voices like thunder. And in their wake would lie fields of dead warriors and smoldering cities.

The tragedy of the Conquest had begun!

Among the conquistadors were a scant few whose awareness of the epochal aspects of their deeds prompted them to record

their experiences. To one such man—Bernal Díaz del Castillo
—history owes a lasting debt of gratitude. Díaz was born in
the Spanish village of Medina del Campo in the fateful year
of 1492. As a young man he journeyed to the Americas in
search of adventure and fortune. He never acquired the wealth
which he sought. He died in Guatemala, a relatively poor land-
owner, at the age of eighty-nine.

Fortunately for historians, Bernal Díaz was a man of keen
perception. He remembered with vivid clarity the dramatic
happenings of his younger years—the months of wandering
along the barren coast of Yucatán on the expeditions of
Córdoba and later Juan de Grijalva; the battles waged in
Aztec Mexico at the side of his revered captain, Hernándo
Cortéz, against the illustrious armies of Montezuma; and the
treacherous marches that carried the tide of conquest into the
disease-ridden jungles of Central America. He was nearing his
eightieth year when he began transcribing the details of the
countless adventures in which he had taken part. In the pref-
ace of his chronicle—*The Discovery and Conquest of Mexico*—he wrote: "I am an old man ... I have lost my sight
and hearing, and, as luck would have it, I have gained nothing
of value to leave to my children and descendants but this my
true story, and they will presently find out what a wonderful
story it is." *

Díaz had conferred a prophetic appraisal on the future
worth of his efforts. His chronicle emerged as one of the few
reliable narratives of the Conquest, a document of inestimable
value in revealing the contrasting natures of the opposing
forces now drawing up in full battle array before history's
silent witness.

* From *The Discovery and Conquest of Mexico* by Bernal Díaz del Castillo.
Copyright 1956 by Farrar, Straus and Cudahy. Used by permission of the publishers, Farrar, Straus and Cudahy, Inc., and Routledge & Kegan Paul, Ltd.

For fifteen days Córdoba's ships proceeded along the Yucatán Peninsula. With their supply of drinking water rapidly diminishing, they went ashore within sight of what appeared to be another town of considerable size. A delegation of Indians dressed in the richly embroidered robes of chieftains assembled to meet them and extended an invitation to visit the city. The treacherous pattern of Catoche was again being enacted, but the certain knowledge that the natives possessed gold inspired otherwise inconceivable risks.

Soon they reached a courtyard enclosed by ornate temples and found themselves surrounded by squadrons of archers and lancers. Slaves came forward carrying bundles of dry reeds which they deposited and set fire to in the plaza. Ten native priests clad in white cotton mantles and whose hair reeked with clotted blood emerged from one of the temples and proceeded to "fumigate" the horrified Spaniards with smoking braziers. ". . . By signs," wrote Bernal Díaz, "they made us understand that we should quit their land before the firewood which they had piled up should burn out, otherwise they would attack and kill us."

Realizing the gravity of their position, the soldiers were not inclined to challenge the priests' direful admonition. ". . . Fear fell upon us," related Díaz, "so we determined to retreat to the coast in good order."

For several weeks more Córdoba's ships continued to explore the western coast of Yucatán. Again in need of fresh water, they disembarked near a third city known as Champoton. Hardly had they beached their longboats when they were surrounded by swarms of warriors, their faces grotesquely painted with black-and-white designs and carrying shields and bright feathered banners. One means of salvation lay open— the faint hope that the Mayan legions, magnificently arrayed in strict formation, would break into panic as the exploding muskets showered death among their ranks.

Hundreds of warriors thronged to the scene, leaving only the open sea as a possible avenue of escape for Córdoba's troops. Their vengeance assumed the overtones of an ominous ritual intended to permanently expel the covetous intruders in their midst: long lines of archers supported by spearsmen arrayed themselves beneath fields of streaming banners and feathered crests. Others behind the lines of battle brought food, drink, fresh supplies of arrows, and lighted fires in which to burn offerings of incense to enraged gods of war.

"We could see," wrote Díaz, "that there were two hundred Indians for every one of us ... and we said to one another, 'let us strengthen our hearts for the fight, and after commending ourselves to God, let us do our best to save our lives.' "

At dawn the siege began. Under a canopy of arrows, darts, and stones hurled from slings, the Mayan legions advanced on the Spaniards' makeshift barricades. Soon they swarmed into their ranks, shooting arrows at close range and slashing with wooden swords edged with obsidian blades. Eighty of the defenders fell wounded in the first onslaught, but their musket fire and steel swords weakened the fury of the attack and the Maya withdrew to safer ground.

With no other means of escape at hand, Córdoba—who had already suffered ten wounds himself—rallied the survivors among his troops in a desperate attempt to reach their waiting boats. Amid loud outcries and a downpour of arrows they fled toward the beach and scrambled aboard their longboats. Some fell during the escape, others were struck down by warriors who pursued them into the water's edge. "Ah!" recalled Díaz, "... to hear the yells, hisses, and cries as the enemy showered arrows on us and hurled lances with all their might, wounding us sorely."

Hardly a man among the survivors was without serious wounds, and two had been carried off alive to be delivered as sacrificial offerings before warrior gods, whose favor was now being sought with new vehemence. With his forces thus shattered and his supplies nearly exhausted, Córdoba ordered his ships to set sail for Cuba. On the return voyage, the wounded lay for weeks suffering the terrible agonies of fever and infection; there was little drinking water, as the casks had been abandoned in the desperate flight from Champoton. "So great was our thirst," lamented Díaz, "that our mouths and tongues were cracked with the dryness, and there was nothing to give us relief. Oh! what hardships one endures when discovering new lands. . . ."

Hernández de Córdoba—who had carried the first threat of conquest to the Mayan nations—died of wounds received at Champoton shortly after his return to Cuba. But his survivors eagerly related tales of the pagan cities, with their weirdly decorous temples containing objects of gold and jade, to listeners whose avarice had not been dulled by the fury of Mayan resistance. Encouraged by the reports, the ambitious Governor Diego Velásquez organized a second expedition to Yucatán and supplied four ships from his personal funds. He placed the fleet under the command of his nephew, Juan de Grijalva. Early in April of 1518, Grijalva's ships, with two hundred and forty soldiers aboard, embarked for Yucatán.

Eighteen days later they touched land at an uncharted island off Yucatán's eastern coast known as Cozumel. Its temples and dwellings had recently been deserted; their inhabitants had withdrawn to observe from unseen hiding places the appearance and behavior of the strange intruders who walked in astonishment among their quarters. From Cozumel the fleet steered in the wake of Córdoba's previous route along the northern coast of the peninsula. Grijalva was scarcely less awed than his predecessor by the realization that he sailed along the frontier of an unknown kingdom.

"Everywhere," wrote William Prescott, "he was struck . . . with the evidences of a higher civilization, especially in the architecture . . ." the astonishing "size and solid materials of the buildings constructed of stone and lime, so different from the frail tenements of reeds and rushes which formed the habitations of the islanders"; the advanced system of agriculture practiced in Yucatán, and "the delicate texture of the cotton garments and gold ornaments of the natives. . . . He was astonished also at the sight of large stone crosses, evidently objects of worship, which he met with in various places. Reminded by these circumstances of his own country, he gave the peninsula the name of 'New Spain.' "

But Grijalva was also to experience the terrifying spectacle of Mayan resentment. Arriving at Champoton, he was greeted by the same fury that brought Córdoba's expedition to a disastrous end. After a furious battle the Spaniards gained access to the city itself only to find it deserted, its streets silent of all but their hushed voices as they surveyed its stone temples and sculptured shrines.

Sailing west from Champoton, the fleet arrived at the mouth of the Río Tabasco, which empties its muddy waters drawn from inland swamps into the Bay of Campeche. Grijalva was curious to explore the river's course; no one before him had penetrated more than a few hundred yards beyond the shore. Utilizing the only feasible means of carrying out his reconnaissance, he crowded his soldiers aboard the two smallest vessels and proceeded inland.

Hardly had they entered the river before the two slowly moving ships were surrounded by canoes laden with heavily armed warriors. Grijalva called out through his interpreters, offering gifts of beads and inviting the Maya to come aboard peaceably. ". . . The Captain told them that we came from a distant country," wrote Díaz, "and were the vassals of a great Emperor named Don Carlos, who had many great lords and chiefs as his vassals, and that they ought to acknowledge him as their lord, and it would be to their advantage to do so, and

that in return for the beads they might bring us some food and
poultry.

"Two of the Indians answered us, and said that they would
bring the food which we asked for, and would barter their
things for ours, but as for the rest, they already had a chief,
that we were only just arrived and knew nothing about them,
and yet we wanted to give them a chief. Let us beware not to
make war on them as we had done at Champoton, for they
had more than three *jiquipiles* of warriors from all the provinces around in readiness (every *jiquipil* numbers eight thousand
men), and they said they were well aware that only a few days
earlier we had killed and wounded more than two hundred
men at Champoton but that they were not weaklings such as
those. . . ."

Grijalva then presented their leaders with strings of beads
and told them his soldiers would camp overnight at the river's
edge to await their return.

"The following day," continued Díaz, "more than thirty
Indians with their chief came to the promontory under the
palm trees where we were camped and brought roasted fish and
fowls, and zapote fruit and maize bread, and braziers with live
coals and incense, and they fumigated us all. Then they spread
on the ground some mats, which here they call *petates,* and over
them a cloth, and they presented some golden jewels, some
were diadems, and others were in the shape of ducks . . . and
other jewels like lizards and three necklaces of hollow beads,
and other articles of gold. . . . They also brought some cloaks
and shirts such as they wear, and said that we must accept these
things in good part as they had no more gold to give us, but
that farther on in the direction of the sunset there was much
gold, and they said 'Colua, Colua, Méjico, Méjico,' but we
did not know what this Colua or Méjico could be. . . ."

The place of which the Mayan traders spoke was the mountainous country to the north, then dominated by the Aztec

nation under the emperor Montezuma. During the three centuries immediately prior to the Conquest the Aztecs had risen from semi-barbaric nomads to the guardians of an eloquent civilization and had extended their domain far beyond the Valley of Mexico in which their impressive capital city of Tenochtitlán was situated. Powerful legions of Aztec knights —arrayed in armor of eagle feathers and jaguar skins, carrying bright-crested shields and lances, and marching to battle amid the din of drums and conch-shell trumpets—had crushed the Totonac, Tlaxcalan, and Olmec nations along Mexico's eastern coast, and overrun the superb Zapotec cities in the south. They had exacted heavy tributes from their subjects and dragged away thousands of captives to be sacrificed on the bloody altars of Tenochtitlán. The Aztec empire had grown rich beyond measure on the spoils of conquest, and by the sixteenth century its rulers were in possession of a military state which rivaled the wealth and splendor of contemporary European nations.

As the stories of Mexico's rich kingdoms continued to unfold, Grijalva determined to track them to their source. He abandoned his plan to explore the Río Tabasco in favor of venturing north along the Mexican coast. Soon Grijalva's fleet came within sight of snow-covered mountains—the volcanic sierras that rise up beyond the coast of Veracruz toward the Mexican plateau. At almost every turn they were watched by squadrons of warriors brandishing lances, streaming banners, and feathered crests, for their arrival in these waters was not entirely unheralded.

The knowledge of Córdoba's earlier expedition had spread far into the interior of Mexico. Montezuma himself had received the news with profound foreboding: his oracles had perceived the coming of intruders months before. They proclaimed the event as the fulfillment of an ancient prophecy which decreed that a god banished centuries earlier from the

Valley of Mexico, Quetzalcoatl—the venerable Plumed Serpent—would return from the "direction of the sunrise," bringing with him a new order to the Aztec realm. Montezuma
viewed the appearance of the strange ships and the bearded
men who guided them as a portent of his own abdication in
behalf of the resurrected deity.

Piedras Negras

But the challenge of Mexico was too formidable for the
wearying Juan de Grijalva. Having bartered their trade goods
with coastal Indians in exchange for gold, his ships returned to
Cuba. It remained for the illustrious conqueror, Hernándo
Cortéz, inflamed by Grijalva's discoveries, to march into the
heart of the Aztec empire the following year—in 1519—with
horses and cannon and trample its glories to dust. Cortéz
arrived from the Eastern Sea exactly as the emperor's sages
had foretold. But he was in no way the image of the cherished
Quetzalcoatl—the new order that Cortéz inflicted upon the
vanquished peoples of Mexico was propounded of greed and
the unyielding intolerance of the Spanish Inquisition. While
zealous friars—following in the wake of Cortéz' military victories—pursued the task of resurrecting "heathens" from
savagery, the temples of their fallen gods were looted of gold
and their lands were carved into grants on which they would
work as slaves. Such was the ominous pattern that was slowly
enveloping the civilizations of the American Indian.

For two decades after Cortéz had brought Mexico and most
of Central America under Spanish supremacy, Yucatán re-

mained firmly in the possession of the Maya. Crown colonies were established in Chiapas, Tabasco, Guatemala, and Honduras, but no serious inroads had been effected in the peninsula itself. The previous expeditions of Córdoba and Grijalva had been more concerned with preliminary explorations than actual conquest, but the rising tides of Spanish fortunes in the New World now made Yucatán's subjugation both logical and desirable.

Francisco de Montejo had commanded one of Grijalva's ships during the expedition of 1518. Later he abandoned his adventurous life in the Americas and returned to his native Spain. Some years thereafter he petitioned Charles the Fifth with a detailed plan to establish a permanent colony in Yucatán. He was granted a royal contract to insure him a proper share of whatever wealth such a venture might provide the king's treasury. With the necessary financial backing supplied by the sale of his wife's estate, he departed from Spain in 1527 with three ships and an army of hopeful followers.

Fortune did not favor the ambitious Montejo. His first colony which took root on the mainland opposite Cozumel Island had to be abandoned in the wake of an acute scourge of fever. Nor had he reckoned with the threats of mutiny among his discouraged troops and the carefully plotted resistance of the natives who permitted the survivors of his ill-fated colony to journey deep into the mainland before unleashing their hostility. Eventually Montejo exacted the submission of several Mayan chieftains to his cause, but the persistent ravages of disease, starvation, and unpacified natives forced him to relinquish his hard-won foothold on the peninsula. Montejo's hope of acquiring land, slaves, and riches had long since faded; his deeper ambition—that of proclaiming himself conqueror of Yucatán—was temporarily abandoned.

In 1531 he again attempted to bring the vast territories of the Yucatán Peninsula into the growing dominions of New

Spain. He had assembled a sizable army and several vessels with which to launch a new attack from the direction of Campeche. Aiding him was his son, Francisco de Montejo the Younger, who immediately set out with a sizable force to explore and colonize the northern extremity of the peninsula. After a difficult journey inland he succeeded in establishing a colony at Chichén Itzá, once the most important city in the upper half of Yucatán. But Montejo's new venture held no more promise of success than his previous attempt: six months later the Indians united to defy the one-sided terms under which they were being forced to serve the Spaniards' ambitious undertaking. Montejo's garrison was besieged and his army driven to the coast.

By 1540 virtually all of Mexico, along with vast portions of Central and South America, was under Spanish domination. Certain Mayan tribes, particularly those in western Yucatán, had concluded that further resistance was useless and had submitted, if somewhat reluctantly, in the hope of winning leniency from their overlords. It was with mounting confidence that Montejo the Younger—empowered by his father to fulfill the terms of his royal contract—laid plans for a third attempt to penetrate the inter recesses of Yucatán and crush the remaining strongholds of native resistance.

In 1541 he invaded the peninsula with a force of four hundred men equipped with horses and cannon. Messengers were sent to the Mayan lords entreating them to submit peaceably to Spanish rule; a few provinces yielded without further hostility to what now seemed an inevitable fate. But those in the north, especially a rebellious group known as the Ah Canul, refused to acknowledge the terms of surrender. Montejo then divided his army in half and dispatched one hundred and sixty men under the command of his cousin to crush the dissenting lords.

At the end of a tortuous journey the ragged troop of conquistadors—thirsty and half-starved—arrived at the city of T'ho, where the Ah Canul chieftains had assembled a sizable army to meet them. In a pitched battle against overwhelming odds, the Spanish routed the Mayan legions and gained the submission of the Ah Canul. A garrison was established at T'ho as a preliminary step toward the founding of a permanent settlement. An urgent request for reinforcements was sent to the younger Montejo in Campeche, who immediately set out for T'ho to consolidate the foothold gained by his cousin's victory.

The phenomenal success of the Spanish at T'ho had the effect of a stunning deathblow to the spirit of the Maya. Many previously hostile provinces now reconsidered the surrender of their sovereignty, looking upon the unfortunate turn of events as being the will of their gods. A significant drama then occurred which was to have a shattering effect on the unity of the remaining provinces. On the plains surrounding T'ho there appeared throngs of Indians accompanying a chieftain borne aloft on a feather-decked litter. The Spanish garrison prepared for what they believed would be an attempt to regain the city, but as the warriors drew nearer the chief raised his hand in a gesture of peace. He presented himself to Montejo as the Lord Tutul Xiu, ruler of Mani, then the most powerful province in northern Yucatán. He expressed his respect for the Spaniards and offered the submission of his army to their cause.

A valuable prize had fallen to Montejo. With the support of the influential Tutul Xiu, he was able to obtain the surrender of all but the easternmost Mayan provinces. In 1542 he founded a "Noble and Loyal" city upon the ruins of T'ho, calling it Merída.

Shortly thereafter, the most remote areas of Yucatán fell under the heel of Spanish domination. With the defeat of its straggling armies, the last vestige of the once magnificent Mayan empire was plunged into ruin.

CHAPTER 2

A Civilization Is Forgotten

FROM the outset of Spanish supremacy in the New World the relegation of the Indians to slavery was an accepted practice. "Laborers" were apportioned among the recipients of land grants, and there were few laws to prevent landowners from obtaining additional slaves by any method expedient to their needs. Certain systems of bondage—more subtle and less easily recognizable as such—survived until the late nineteenth century.

In Yucatán thousands of Maya were transplanted from their villages to the estates of *encomenderos,* who, because of the decree of an unseen monarch in a distant country, laid claim to their ancestral lands. A strictly enforced system of tributes was imposed upon them, and expressions of disloyalty brought severe punishment at the hands of overlords who looked upon their servants as "children of the devil."

From a native chronicle written shortly after the Conquest —the *Books of Chilam Balam*—came a revealing summation of the fate which had overtaken the Maya: ". . . it was the beginning of tribute, the beginning of church dues, the beginning of strife with purse snatching, the beginning of strife with guns, the beginning of strife by trampling of people, the beginning of robbery with violence, the beginning of debts enforced by false testimony, the beginning of individual strife, the beginning of vexation."

With implacable fanaticism the Spanish went about the task

of eradicating Mayan culture and traditions. Temples erected to the once-powerful gods who had inspired the brilliant achievements of Mayan civilization were pulled down, their altars and sculptured images smashed, and their further veneration forbidden under threat of harsh penalties. Churches were often constructed on the sites of former temples—tended by Dominican and Franciscan friars whose duty it was to hold aloft the virtues of Christendom before their spiritual wards.

But the ancient beliefs were not easily uprooted. What manner of men were these Spaniards who wrought unspeakable cruelty while spreading the teachings of a god they extolled as benevolent? And the Maya fled deep into the sheltering jungle by night, gathering in deserted temples to make offerings before smuggled idols and invoke the wrath of their gods on the invaders.

Montejo's victory brought the yoke of oppression upon Yucatán with irrevocable finality. The Mayan nations had been crushed, their cities reduced to ruins, the profound accomplishments of their civilization committed to obscurity. It remained now to blot the legacy of the past from the memory of the living Maya, to obliterate the values and traditions by which they had lived for centuries. The task fell largely to one man—a religious zealot whose curious complexity made of him both a relentless assassin and a devoted scholar of all things Mayan.

In 1549 a Franciscan monk named Diego de Landa arrived in Yucatán from Spain to serve in the monastery of Izamal. The spirit of the Inquisition burned brightly in the young cleric's determination to perform his duties. Wherever he traveled during frequent crusades that carried him to remote corners of the peninsula, he saw to it that all vestiges of the native religion were destroyed and proclaimed that anyone caught worshiping heathen gods be severely beaten and made to suffer the harsh penalties by which pagans were "cleansed."

In spite of Landa's efforts, evidence of the Indians' faith in their deeply rooted beliefs continued to manifest itself. It was still the venerable deities of the sun, rain, and fertility to whom the Maya turned in secret when planting their fields; and the supreme Lord Itzamna and the mighty Kukulcan in whose hidden temples they sought vengeance for their grievous plight. Friar de Landa was enraged by the stubborn refusal of his subjects to abandon their traditions; he looked about for new methods of impressing upon the Maya the invalidity of their heritage. Such an opportunity presented itself when he marched, cross in hand, into the town of Mani—formerly the home of the powerful Tutul Xiu dynasty. Because of its prominence in Mayan affairs there was assembled at Mani a library made up of books written by native priests prior to the Conquest. On discovering this valuable archive, Landa committed an act of wanton destruction which was to rob future scholars of the most potentially valuable source of information to survive into historic times. He ordered that the books be brought to the town plaza and publicly burned!

On the prescribed day the disastrous auto-da-fé was carried out. Because, as Landa wrote, the books "contained nothing in which there was not to be seen superstition and lies of the devil, we burned them all...." An archaeological treasure, the recorded knowledge of centuries which had permitted the Maya to achieve unparalleled eloquence among the high civilizations of the New World, lay ruined in the smoldering embers of Landa's terrible deed.

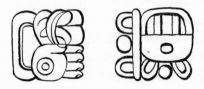

Palenque

Among the ancient Maya literature had reached a high degree of development. Their books—or codices, as they are called—consisted of a single strip of parchment pounded from vegetable fiber strengthened by the application of a natural gum substance. The entire parchment was coated on both sides with white lime. Onto this surface priests laboriously inscribed complex hieroglyphic characters, coloring them with vegetable and mineral paints. The manuscript then was folded and enclosed between wooden or leather covers, making a single volume or codex not unlike a modern book in appearance.

Unfortunately only three such Mayan codices are known to have survived to the present day. In 1739 the so-called Dresden Codex—which deals largely with astronomical calculations—was discovered in Vienna and later acquired by the State Library in Dresden, Germany. During the last half of the nineteenth century sections of two manuscripts of Mayan origin were found in Spain. Examination showed them to be part of the same document, the Codex Tro-Cortesianus, a study of astrology used by priests. It is preserved in the Museum of Archaeology and History in Madrid. The third codex is in the possession of the Bibliothèque Nationale in Paris where it came to light in 1860 in a box of forgotten documents. Large portions of this third codex, designated as the Codex Peresianus, are missing, but the remaining sections contain lucid descriptions of certain deities and religious ceremonials.

Valuable though these codices have been to archaeological research, they shed no light whatsoever on actual historical occurrences. What priceless records illuminating the history of Mayan civilization from its obscured origin through the successive periods of its development and decline were destroyed by Landa's auto-da-fé will never be known. The archive at Mani might well have clarified many of the puzzling enigmas revealed by later archaeological research. Almost certainly the ravaged manuscripts would have been of enormous value in

deciphering the hieroglyphic writing with which the Maya
recorded the events of their time. Scarcely one third of these
glyphs can be accurately interpreted at present—those pertaining to astronomical and calendrical computations, the day,
month, and year signs, and numerical symbols. But the vast
majority of Mayan inscriptions remain unintelligible to modern scholars.

Even without the lost codices, the collapsed temples and
palaces, the shattered stairways, and weathered stelae or date-
markers found in ruined Mayan cities are covered with the
curiously fashioned hieroglyphic figures that withhold so much
information which archaeologists would like to recover. As
yet, however, there is no key with which to unravel their meaning, no Rosetta Stone such as that which solved the enigma of
Egyptian hieroglyphics. And this fact is made more lamentable
by the realization that the Maya were the only peoples of pre-
Columbian America to evolve a complex written language considerably beyond the point of simple pictographic representations.

Another indication of Mayan literary prowess has fallen
into the hands of scholars by a curious route. After the Conquest, the natives were taught to transpose their own language
into Spanish. Once the Maya were able to read and write, the
propagation of Christian teachings would move more rapidly;
it was to that end alone that the friars painstakingly instructed
their subjects. It was inevitable, however, that this knowledge
was put to use in recording matters of concern to native chroniclers who were justly alarmed by the rapid passing of their
heritage.

A few of these post-Conquest documents have survived to
convey with eloquent simplicity the reflections of their authors
concerning their history and traditions. From the Guatemalan
highlands came the sacred book of the Quiché Maya—the
Popul Vuh—recounting the myths, cosmology, and religion of

Quiché people who had formerly dominated the southern high-lands. Scribes of a neighboring people compiled a similar document known as *The Annals of the Cakchiquels*. And an important collection of manuscripts bearing on the history of northern Yucatán was assembled in the so-called *Books of Chilam Balam,* named for a class of priests (or Chilam) famous for their prophetic powers and delvings into the supernatural.

Again, however, these documents elude the more perplexing questions raised by the cumulative findings of archaeological study. The disquieting fact looms large: the few existing fragments of Mayan literature do little more than confirm our suspicion that the Maya were masters of that art as well. Scholars are almost totally without written sources which bear directly upon scientific contentions—records of early migrations, the founding of cities, social and political evolution, warfare, and commerce. Most of what the Maya themselves may have written about the momentous attainments of their civilization is but another of the fathomless voids that challenge modern research; owing in large measure to Diego de Landa, whose appearance among the Maya extinguished even the hope of preserving the recollection of former glories in the wake of their military failure to regain them completely.

Palenque

Landa's career followed two widely divergent routes. To better equip himself for his mission, he had plunged into a thorough study of Mayan culture immediately upon his arrival in Yucatán. Such a pursuit could hardly have failed to excite his curiosity to a point beyond the specific purpose of his delvings. He spent much of his time in the company of nobles of the Xiu and Cocom families, questioning them at length on matters of history, folklore, mythology, and religion. Wherever he traveled throughout Yucatán he collected information concerning every facet of native life. Unknown to the zealous Friar Landa, he was unwittingly to emerge from these pursuits as the first eminent scholar of the archaic traditions he sought to abolish.

About the year 1566 Landa began writing a monumental history of Yucatán based upon his earlier studies. He may have had in mind the idea of compiling a guide to instruct younger missionaries in the subtleties of spreading the faith among the Maya. Others are of the opinion that Landa undertook the project in the hope of lessening official criticism of his actions at Mani, although he could hardly have offered his history as a substitute for the priceless Mayan books he had plundered. Whatever his purpose may have been, Landa's efforts resulted in a document of singular importance to future research. His manuscript, entitled *Relación de las cosas de Yucatán,* contains a wealth of detailed information relative to numerous previously unrecorded aspects of Mayan culture. It is among the few historical documents with which investigators have been able to correlate certain archaeological findings.

Landa's work was a monumental undertaking. It probed into every facet of the daily lives, customs, religious beliefs, and history drawn by him from the still-lucid memory of his spiritual subjects. Its pages are filled with laborious descriptions of the rich pageantry and folklore by which the Maya had sought to animate and enshrine their traditions in times past.

Especially was he concerned with finding a means by which Mayan hieroglyphics could be deciphered. He noted such items of importance to present-day archaeologists as the names and identifying hieroglyphs for the days, months, and years on which their calendar was based. But his efforts to devise an "alphabet" for reading the non-astronomical inscriptions—drawings of figures or objects that when pronounced in the native tongue bore sounds similar to the characters of the Spanish alphabet—have proved of relatively little value in deciphering the remaining glyphs.

Except for Landa's initial studies, virtually nothing would be known of Mayan culture as it existed at the time of the Conquest. In Middle America, as elsewhere throughout the vast territories of New Spain, the manifestations of high civilizations which had flourished there in centuries past held little fascination for the fortune-hungry colonists. Their primary concern lay in expanding the political and economic frontiers of their holdings. Of what value were the ruined cities and forgotten achievements of "devil worshipers"?

By no means had a single objective inspired the age of exploration and conquest which had overtaken the Western Hemisphere. Men inflamed by military ambition, dreams of personal fortune, religious dogmatism, and the allurement of pure adventure had united for the westward advance. Their faith was twofold: God, and the new acquisitions of Western Civilization—steel and gunpowder. And preceding events of European history had instilled in them the belief that to whoever mastered the effective application of the latter, even the most apparent fate was alterable. So equipped, a handful of Spanish soldiers had challenged a continent and emerged victorious.

But the Maya had fallen in defeat not because of the superiority of Spanish armament alone. Indeed, the outcome might have been considerably different had not internal subterfuge thrown the Maya into a state of decline long before the threat of Spanish invasion. Beginning approximately in 1450, civil unrest and violence had erupted throughout their realm. Yucatán was the scene of almost continuous fighting between the powerful ruling families of the Cocom and the Tutul Xiu; in Guatemala the Quiché warred with the Cakchiquel nation for control of the highlands. Revolution, political assassinations, and intrigue beset their once-peaceful domain. Secular power formerly held by a central governing authority fell into the covetous hands of independent chieftains. Militarism supplanted the constructive endeavors of earlier centuries; there was little time for creative activity or the pursuit of higher learning. Even the fields were often deserted by farmers conscripted into military service.

Like acts of punishment from the gods, a series of catastrophes overtook the Maya in the midst of their tribulations. A severe hurricane laid waste vast portions of Yucatán. In its wake a pestilence ravaged their fields, and a plague swept through the populace—disasters unlike any the Maya had ever experienced before. A cryptic chant from the *Books of Chilam Balam* sang of the happenings that would herald the end of their age:

> "*Eat, eat, thou hast bread;*
> *Drink, drink, thou hast water;*
> *On that day, dust possesses the earth,*
> *On that day, a blight is on the face of the earth,*
> *On that day, a cloud rises,*
> *On that day, a strong man seizes the land,*
> *On that day, things fall to ruin,*
> *On that day, the tender leaf is destroyed,*
> *On that day, the dying eyes are closed,*
> *On that day, three signs are on the tree,*
> *On that day, three generations hang there,*
> *On that day, the battle flag is raised,*
> *And they are scattered afar in the forests.*" *

* *Book of Chilam Balam of Tizimin.* Ms. Original in Mexico, D. F. Photographed by Teobert Maler; Gates reproduction made for Dr. S. G. Morley. Prophecy translated by D. G. Brinton, *Maya Chronicles,* in Library of Aboriginal American Literature, No. 1. Philadelphia: 1882.

History's eternal drama had again been enacted. Mayan civilization—the most eloquent expression of higher attainments in pre-Columbian America—had been destroyed, utterly obliterated from the stage of human affairs. All the Maya had accomplished lay buried and forgotten in their dead cities, engulfed by the primeval jungle out of which they had been spawned at some undisclosed time in the past.

For the living Maya two paths of survival lay open: the pallid existence of slavery, or the alternative that claimed the thousands who sought escape from oppression—to abandon the knowledge of engineering, mathematics, astronomy, literature, and the faint recollections of a Golden Era—to live like progeny of the Stone Age "scattered afar in the forests."

It remained for men possessed of insatiable curiosity to reclaim the achievements of the Maya from permanent oblivion; men of less worldly ambitions than their Spanish predecessors to whom the quest for knowledge was as enticing as the lure of gold.

CHAPTER 3

John Lloyd Stephens:
The Cities Come to Light

IN 1836 a meeting occurred in London which was to bear profoundly upon the enigma of the forgotten Mayan cities. John Lloyd Stephens,* an American whose career as a lawyer had given way to his predilection for travel and the study of antiquities, was introduced to the English artist, Frederick Catherwood. Prior to their meeting the course of their lives had been conspicuously similar, for both men were deeply immersed in the study of Near Eastern archaeology.

Stephens was born in Shrewsbury, New Jersey, in 1805. He entered Columbia University to prepare for a legal career, but the confinement of a settled existence did not satisfy his more adventurous ambitions. He was insatiably curious about distant corners of the globe and determined to delay his earlier intentions in order to travel. Indeed, in the years to come John Lloyd Stephens became the most celebrated traveler of his day and recorded the incidents of his wanderings in a series of highly successful books.

Frederick Catherwood had long been a serious student of classical sculpture and architecture. He knew well the ruins of Greece and the mighty structures of pharaonic Egypt. He had

---

* A recent account and analysis of Stephens' explorations and discoveries is contained in *Maya Explorer: John Lloyd Stephens and the Lost Cities of Central America and Yucatán,* by Victor Wolfgang Von Hagen (Norman: University of Oklahoma Press, 1947).

visited Mt. Sinai, Petra, and made detailed drawings of the Hellenistic city of Baalbek. He was unusually adept at rendering accurate reproductions of architecture and stone sculpture. Unlike many of his contemporaries—who immersed their art in the careless fantasies of romanticism—Catherwood tempered his innate mysticism with the unerring pen and critical eye of a skilled draftsman. To him every detail of design, every intention of the artisans whose works he copied, demanded faithful reproduction.

The fact that Stephens was guided by the same integrity in his literary observations made their meeting a fortunate one in view of events yet to come. Both men were to play singularly important roles in bringing to light before a skeptical world the achievements of the ancient Maya.

Stephens had returned to New York from London in 1836 at the conclusion of an extended tour of the Near East. He opened a law office, began writing a book about his adventures, and plunged with vigor into an impending presidential campaign in support of Martin Van Buren.

Before leaving London, however, he had stumbled upon an account written by an officer in the Spanish Army some time near the close of the eighteenth century—a Captain Antonio del Río—which claimed the existence of a large ruined city known as Palenque in the jungles of southern Mexico. The possibility that a ruin such as Del Río had described might actually exist never completely left Stephens' consciousness— the thought was far too intriguing!

Interest in such matters was further heightened by the appearance between 1831 and 1837 of a series of books entitled *The Antiquities of Mexico,* the life work of one Lord Kingsborough. For years prior to their publication, he had relentlessly tracked every fragment of information on pre-Columbian civilization known to exist in Europe. His works contained detailed studies of architectural remains and sculpture thus far discovered in the Americas, along with superb reproductions of known codices. Out of the jumbled text loomed its author's firm conviction that the aboriginal inhabitants of the Americas were, in fact, survivors of the lost Tribes of Israel. But Kingsborough's admirable attempt to prove his belief became his denouement—he was cast into debtors' prison unable to bear the staggering expense of his publications.

Several years later a friend showed Stephens a portfolio containing the work of Count Jean Frédéric Waldeck, a German artist and soldier of fortune who had recently visited southern Mexico and the Yucatán Peninsula. In it were elaborate drawings of the mysterious ruined cities which Waldeck had found scattered throughout the vicinity of his travels. At once the weirdly conceived animal and human figures, the intricate architectural embellishments upon buildings of seemingly herculean proportions, excited Stephens' imagination. He began to probe deeper into the writings of early historians and the few travelers who had penetrated these virtually unknown regions for every fragment of evidence that further hinted of archaeological remains. Finally, his curiosity was inflamed beyond resistance by an article that appeared in the *Proceedings of the American Antiquarian Society*. It confirmed the discovery of a vast ruined city in Honduras known as Copán. Stephens announced his intention of exploring the depths of the Central American jungle to obtain positive proof or denial of the existence of these rumored monuments of ancient grandeurs.

It was not surprising that his announcement touched off a flurry of wild speculation. Public fancy was captivated by Stephens' romantic mission of discovery, but historians and antiquarians (the archaeologists of their day) were openly skeptical of its merits. The then relatively new science of archaeology—which by the middle of the nineteenth century was receiving almost constant impetus from findings in the

Near East—had never been seriously applied to the American continents. Napoleon's invasion of Egypt in 1789 had brought the astounding antiquities scattered along the Nile to the attention of European scholars. Champollion had begun his efforts to decipher the inscriptions of the Rosetta Stone; Paul Emile Botta was uncovering the city of Nineveh; and Austen Layard was probing the remains of the once-illustrious Assyrian empire. The world looked to the Mediterranean lands, awaiting with mounting curiosity the next discovery in the fascinating chain of events which gave rise to the science of archaeology.

But so far as the Western Hemisphere was concerned, scholarly consensus rigidly held to the belief that the American Indians had at no point in their history progressed beyond the condition of barest savagery. In spite of contrary documentary evidence dating from the Conquest, the suggestion that aboriginal civilizations of the highest order had once flourished in the southern half of the Americas was utterly untenable to the majority of historians.

It was obvious that in the event his quest proved successful, Stephens would need documentary proof of his findings. No one was better qualified to provide such material than his friend Catherwood, whose superb drawings and maps of Near Eastern ruins had achieved considerable recognition. Eager for an opportunity to explore previously unknown areas, Catherwood promptly accepted Stephens' offer to accompany him. Thus two men—each gifted with limitless curiosity and exceptional abilities in their respective media of expression—united to challenge the trackless Central American wilderness in search of a lost civilization.

On the eve of their departure Stephens was awarded the post of United States ambassador to Central America, a position for which he had applied upon the sudden death of the former minister. The occurrence was a fortunate one; the countries he intended to visit were locked in the midst of violent internal disturbances. Rebellious armies were battling for political control of Central America's dawning republics. All attempts to preserve law and order during the strife had broken down, and opposing factions within the contending armies were fighting among themselves. The territory—hazardous enough under normal conditions—teemed with marauding bandits and smugglers. It was a situation hardly encouraging to foreign travelers entering upon a purely scholarly quest, though Stephens hoped that his diplomatic license would afford some degree of immunity from the dangers that lay ahead.

In October of 1839 the explorers embarked for Belize in British Honduras. From there they boarded a steamer bound for Lake Izabal, some distance inland from the eastern coast of Guatemala, along the Río Dulce. At the port of Izabal, situated on the southern edge of the lake, one could hire guides for the overland journey across a jagged barrier known as Mico Mountain into the war-torn hinterlands of Guatemala and points beyond.

By mule they traveled deeper into the thickly forested mountains—toward what they hoped would be the ancient city of Copán. Still there was no assurance that they had not set off in pursuit of a fantasy. Once surrounded by the cavernous rain forest that blanketed their route, desolate and entangled beyond anything he had previously suspected, Stephens had sufficient reason to question the wisdom of his undertaking. Was it possible that a civilization had once flourished in these hostile surroundings? Would it not be wise to review the appraisals of scholarly opinion and retreat from so unlikely a quest? Before them lay an immutable void, an unexplored realm suited only to its primal inhabitants—its myriad insects, exotic birds, monkeys, and the thick-bodied iguanas that thrashed about nervously in the underbrush, peering with antique eyes at the men and laden beasts who shattered the silence of their primeval existence.

Stephens wrote of the hazards that befell them almost from the outset of their journey: "The ascent began precipitously and by way of an extraordinary passage, a narrow gulley worn by the tracks of mules and the washing of mountain torrents. It was so deep that the sides were higher than our heads, and so narrow that we could barely pass through without touching them. Our whole caravan moved singly through this muddy defile. The muleteers scattered among them and on the bank above, extricating the mules as they stuck fast, raising them as they fell, arranging their cargoes, cursing, shouting, and lashing them on; if one stopped, all behind were blocked up, unable to turn. Any sudden start pressed us against the sides of the gulley, and there was no small danger of getting a leg crushed. Emerging from this defile, we came to deep mudholes, and projecting roots of trees, which added to the difficulty of a steep ascent. The heavy rains . . . had deluged the mountain, and it was in the worst state it could be and still be passable; sometimes it was not passable at all. . . . The woods were of impenetrable thickness and we could see nothing but the detestable path before us." *

Eventually they entered higher terrain less formidable to penetrate. But the physical rigors of their journey soon gave way to the political exigencies of the times. At Comatán, a few miles short of their destination, Stephens' party was "arrested" and held in confinement throughout a precarious night of negotiations during which Stephens' refusal to yield to the unreasonable demands of their captors almost brought the expedition to a disastrous end. At last the matter was resolved and they proceeded to the sparsely inhabited Indian settlement of

* *Incidents of Travel in Central America, Chiapas, and Yucatán,* edited by Richard L. Predmore. New Brunswick, New Jersey: Rutgers University Press. Copyright 1949 by the Trustees of Rutgers College in New Jersey.

Copán. Here again the appearance of outsiders was an unwelcome event.

No one could tell them the whereabouts of ruins such as Stephens described, but all agreed that the one man who might be of assistance was Don Gregorio—a suspicious, ill-tempered half-breed who was the self-styled "mayor" of the desolate village. Don Gregorio received Stephens with cold indifference. Neither gestures of friendship nor offers of money could alter his menacing disposition, and he finally consented to help only in the hope of ridding himself of his unwanted visitors. He knew of an Indian who could lead them to the ruins; the explorers were allowed to camp at his hacienda until arrangements could be made for his services.

Early the next morning Stephens and Catherwood, accompanied by their newly acquired guide, set off by mule into the fathomless green void. Soon the underbrush was so thick that it became necessary to proceed on foot along a path cleared with machetes. When at last they emerged at the edge of the Copán River, a high stone wall thickly encrusted with vines was clearly visible on the opposite bank.

Hurriedly they forged the river and struggled up a weathered stairway leading to the wall's summit. They found themselves standing on a terrace from which vestiges of still other stone structures were barely discernible in the tangled jungle below. Stephens and his companions descended into its shadowy depths and stood in the midst of wonders exceeding their wildest expectations.

Scattered about the jungle floor were tall stone columns, some standing erect, others fallen over or broken, their surfaces deeply etched with sculptured figures of animal and human forms together with what appeared to be inscriptions. Huge stone altars covered with carved effigies of richly costumed men and animal-like masks lay half-buried in the earth at their feet. Pyramid-shaped structures reached up through the treetops, barely visible under the thick mantle of jungle growth in which they were enveloped. The surfaces of the buildings and the stairways leading to their flat-topped summits were shattered by roots of trees and vines that grew between the fissured stones. Great monolithic heads of jaguars and fanged serpents had fallen from their façades—images of the gods in whose veneration the once-magnificent temples had been raised. Everywhere the explorers looked were miracles frozen in the crumbled monuments of ancient Copán!

It was obvious that the mysterious city had not only been a center of considerable size, but the scene of past achievements totally outside the environs of previous knowledge. Its discovery was of *monumental importance!* Stephens' first view of the ruins left little question in his mind that prevailing academic dogma—which had stubbornly refused to retreat from its certainty that the American Indian had never raised himself from barbarism—had been totally demolished.

"Who were the people that built this city?" Stephens later wrote. "In the ruined cities of Egypt, even in the long-lost Petra, the stranger knows the story of the people whose vestiges he finds around him. America, say historians, was peopled by savages; but savages never reared these structures, savages never carved these stones.... Architecture, sculpture, and painting, all the arts which embellish life, had flourished in this overgrown forest; orators, warriors, and statesmen, beauty, ambition, and glory had lived and passed away, and none knew that such things had been, or could tell of their past existence....

"The city was desolate. No remnant of this race hangs round the ruins, with traditions handed down from father to son and from generation to generation. It lay before us like a shattered bark in the midst of the ocean, her masts gone, her name effaced, her crew perished, and none to tell whence she came, to whom she belonged, how long on her voyage, or what caused her destruction—her lost people to be traced only by some fancied resemblance in the construction of the vessel, and, perhaps, never to be known at all. . . . All was mystery, dark, impenetrable mystery, and every circumstance increased it. In Egypt the colossal skeletons of gigantic temples stand in unwatered sands in all the nakedness of desolation; but there an immense forest shrouds the ruins, hiding them from sight, heightening the impression and moral effect, and giving an intensity and almost wildness to the interest."

Indeed, at the time Stephens could scarcely have comprehended the full significance of his discovery. Before him lay expressions in stone unlike anything he had previously encountered. Here were manifestations of creative activity wholly self-contained, ideals held fast in stone of a people whose origin was lost in obscurity and whose history was linked to no other known civilization. Stephens was not alone in his evaluation. It had been said before by one who had happened upon Copán: *"The genii who attended on King Solomon seem to have been the artists."*

Exploring the ruins presented formidable difficulties. Paths had to be opened through the site, the monuments had to be cleared of underbrush, some that had fallen over had to be raised again in order to expose them to view. Stephens recruited a number of Indian laborers from the village and soon the work of reclaiming the forgotten city from its jungle grave was under way.

"It is impossible to describe the interest with which I explored these ruins," wrote Stephens of their first days at the site. "The ground was entirely new; there were no guide-books or guides; the whole was virgin soil. We could not see ten yards before us, and never knew what we should stumble upon next. At one time we stopped to cut away branches and vines, which concealed the face of a monument . . . a sculptured corner of which protruded from the earth. I leaned over with breathless anxiety while the Indians worked, and an eye, an ear, a foot, or a hand was disentombed; and when the machete rang against the chiseled stone, I pushed the Indians away and cleared out the loose earth with my hands. The beauty of the sculpture, the solemn stillness of the woods disturbed only by the scrambling of monkeys and the chattering of parrots, the desolation of the city, and the mystery that hung over it, all created an interest higher, if possible, than I had ever felt among the ruins of the Old World."

Working with great difficulty, the explorers surveyed the visible structures and attempted to map the outlines of obliterated remains as accurately as possible. The principal complex of Copán's structures was situated atop a terraced acropolis covering twelve acres and rising to a height of one hundred and twenty-five feet. Crowning this artificial platform was a massive pyramid that rose up in a series of gradual terraces to a flat summit. At its western base was a courtyard enclosed by smaller temples. To the east was yet another plaza surrounded by numerous fallen structures. At one end of this Eastern Court stood a temple, the doorway of which was flanked by crouching human figures supporting massive wreaths of ornamental sculpture.

Perhaps the greatest single achievement of Copán's builders was the so-called Hieroglyphic Stairway leading down from the acropolis complex toward what is now known as the Great Plaza at the northern limit of the city. The passage was thirty-three feet wide and consisted of sixty-two steeply inclined steps. Every stone used in its construction had glyphs deeply etched on its surface, and the entire stairway was composed of almost two thousand individual glyphs.

Many of the stones from the collapsed buildings and almost every sizable fragment of sculpture bore these same peculiar glyphic figures; they appeared in infinite variety, but always they were present. Stephens was certain they were linguistic

characters rather than purely decorative motifs—hieroglyphs
by means of which Copán's inhabitants had intended to per-
petuate their history and accumulated knowledge. The idea also
occurred to him that the sculptured columns or "idols," scattered about the courtyard, had been erected to commemorate
specific historical events or the passing of certain time intervals.
Later investigations were to verify both assumptions.

Equally intriguing to Stephens was the atmosphere about the
ruins which led one to speculate that the whole place was the
creation of sorcerers rather than men of ordinary gifts—an
impression evoked not only by its jungle setting, the eerie cries
of phantom-quick monkeys uttered from their unseen perches,
the vivid sensation that one had traversed backward through
history to reach the ancient city, but by something more tangible. Copán did not appear to have been a center whose inspiration was that of market places and commerce. Rather, it was
a city of celestial monuments, of angular pyramids and cham-
bered temples from which the faces of nameless gods had
looked out upon ceremonial courtyards—a meeting place of
nobles, high priests, and oracles concerned with matters of
science, art, philosophy, and metaphysics. The entire city was
like a gigantic shrine. Stephens remarked that the sculptural
figuration most frequently encountered was death's-heads:
"There were whole rows of them on the outer wall, adding
gloom to the mystery of the place, keeping death and the grave
before the eyes of the living, presenting the idea of a holy city
—the Mecca or Jerusalem of an unknown people."

No sooner was the systematic exploration well under way
than a serious problem of diplomacy arose, touched off by the
growing resentment of Don Gregorio. "While we had been
busy with our own affairs," wrote Stephens, "we had but little
idea what a sensation we were causing in the village. Not satis-
fied with getting us out of his house, Don Gregorio wanted to
get us out of the neighborhood. Unluckily, besides his instinc-

tive dislike, we had offended him in drawing off some of his workmen by the high prices which as strangers we were obliged to pay. He had begun to look upon us as rivals, saying everywhere that we were suspicious characters, that we had been the cause of disturbing the peace of Copán and of introducing soldiers and the war into the neighborhood. In confirmation of this, two Indians who passed through the village reported that we had escaped from imprisonment, had been chased to the borders of Honduras by a detachment of twenty-five soldiers . . . and that if we had been taken, we would have been shot. The alcalde who had been drunk ever since our arrival, resolved to visit us, to solve the doubts of the village, and to take whatever measures the presence of such dangerous persons and the safety of the country might require. But his doughty purpose was frustrated by a ludicrous circumstance. We had made it a rule to carry our arms with us to the ruins, and when we returned to the hut to receive his visit, each of us had, as usual, a brace of pistols in his belt and a gun in hand. Our appearance was so formidable that the alcalde was frightened at his own audacity in having thought of catechizing us, and he fairly sneaked off."

Still they were in a precarious position; they were without friends in a country torn by civil unrest, subject to the caprices of irresponsible *politicos*. Furthermore, should anyone question their right to continue the exploration of Copán, they would be without recourse. Something had to be done quickly to counter the mounting apprehension of the local inhabitants. Stephens resolved to purchase the ruins!

The land on which they were situated was owned by one Don José María, a tolerant man by prevailing standards; nor was he wholly disposed to support the inclinations of Don Gregorio. Stephens paid a visit to Don José's home. He emphatically denied the rumors being spread in the village, displayed his diplomatic papers bearing their impressive red seals, and explained the reasons for his interest in the ruined city. "In short," he wrote, "in plain English, I asked him, 'What will you take for the ruins?' I think he was not more surprised than if I had asked to buy his poor old wife. . . ."

After several days of deliberation Don José consented to sell. To him the land was useless—six thousand acres of steaming jungle littered with meaningless carved stones and mounds of rubble. And the price he had been offered—fifty dollars—was irresistible. Amid a pompous display of deeds and credentials, the sale was completed.

Stephens was well pleased with his transaction. The sensation of owning a ruined city in the wilds of Central America had an undeniable enchantment about it. And the whole situation had been brought about by practical necessity—under the circumstances it was good business.

For two weeks Stephens and Catherwood labored to redeem Copán's secrets from the entangling forest. Scarcely an hour passed without revealing some new cause for conjecture—a subtle variation in design or the barely visible outlines of prodigious feats of engineering. Stephens' brain fairly reeled with the mystifying enchantment of his ruined city. Who were its builders? Where had they come from? How had they managed to erect their magnificent structures and carve huge blocks of stone as if they were made of clay? What relics lay entombed in the earth beneath them? And what of the fate of Copán's vanished inhabitants?

Finally it was agreed that Stephens would journey on to Guatemala City to fulfill certain diplomatic obligations, while Catherwood continued working at the site. Stephens' heart was no longer in matters of politics; it was a duty made bearable by the knowledge that once accomplished he would be free to continue his explorations. He was now intent upon seeking the rumored city of Palenque!

Copán

Early in the spring of 1840 the explorers were again launched upon a hazardous quest. Several hundred miles of precipitous terrain separated them from the lowlands of Chiapas where Palenque was said to be located. Slowly they worked their way down from the highlands of Guatemala, through the rain forest and savannahs of southern Mexico, toward a village known as Santo Domingo del Palenque. Weeks later Stephens and Catherwood stumbled into its muddy streets, their one thought being to recover from the exhaustion which by now had robbed them, momentarily at least, of even their curiosity for ruined cities.

But the idea of long-dead temples and palaces lying about in the thick jungle which enveloped them soon revived their determination. And when they were finally led to the magnificent city they could scarcely contain their elation. One glimpse of its crumbled monuments had more than justified the hardships required to reach it. "We saw masses of stones," recalled Stephens. ". . . We spurred up a sharp ascent of fragments, so steep the mules could barely climb it, to a terrace which, like the whole road, was so covered with trees it was impossible to make out the form. . . . Through an opening in the trees we saw the front of a large building richly ornamented with stuccoed figures on the pilasters, curious and elegant, with trees growing close against it, their branches entering the doors; in style and effect it was unique, extraordinary, and mournfully beautiful. We tied our mules to the trees, ascended a flight of stone steps forced apart and thrown down by trees, and entered the palace. For a few moments we ranged along the corridor and into the courtyard, and after the first gaze of eager curiosity was over, went back to the entrance. Standing in the doorway, we fired a *feu-de-joie* of four rounds each, using up the last charge of our firearms. But for this way of giving vent to our satisfaction we should have made the roof of the old palace ring with a hurrah. It was intended, too, for effect upon the Indians, who had probably never heard such a cannonade before, and who, almost like their ancestors in the time of Cortéz, regarded our weapons as instruments which spit lightning. They would, we knew, make such a report in the village as would keep any of their respectable friends from paying us a visit at night."

Palenque's Great Palace afforded them their first opportunity to examine the architectural prowess of its builders. Unlike Copán, whose buildings were almost totally obscured by debris, the most impressive structures at Palenque were standing intact. "We were," wrote Stephens, "for the first time ... in a building erected by the aboriginal inhabitants. It had been standing there before the Europeans knew of the existence of this continent, and we prepared to take up our abode under its roof." It was a massive edifice consisting of numerous chambers arranged around a series of four sunken courtyards. Above it a fifty-foot stone tower rose up in a manner vaguely suggestive of an Oriental pagoda.

A series of unusual stucco reliefs embellished the building's outer pilasters. They appeared to be "portraits" of high priests bedecked in elaborate feathered headdresses and ceremonial costumes. Some of them held a plumed staff in one hand and were attended by seated figures. Despite the ravages of decay, which had eaten away whole sections of the frescoes, Catherwood was spellbound by the sensitivity of their expression, the intricacy of detail, and the beauty of their execution. He worked tirelessly to commit them to paper, fearing they would not survive many more seasons of rain.

For untold centuries these somber figures had peered down from the Palace walls, frozen in moods of rigid solemnity. Others were in attitudes of ecstatic dance, their sandaled feet rising from the ground, their bodies bent gently forward, hands outstretched caressing the fetishes of gods—openmouthed and entranced. Thus had these images of holy men witnessed the flowering of Palenque, whose engineers had erected towering pyramids crowned by exquisitely wrought temples, and constructed gleaming stone causeways across the escarpments separating one portion of the city from another; whose astronomer-priests had studied the heavens and probed the most eternal of mysteries; whose artisans had fashioned immortal reflections in stone. And they had watched, too, as the passing centuries awarded the deeds of their vanished subjects to the jungle. . . .

It was soon apparent that Palenque had been an immense city. As far as Stephens wandered in every direction were the unmistakable vestiges of its buildings and monuments. At one corner of the Palace a mound of weathered stones rose up under a mantle of jungle verdure. Stephens was able to discern the outline of steps leading to its summit. With Indians wielding machetes ahead of them, he and Catherwood struggled up the steep incline until they stood at the entrance of a temple whose lavish ornamentation struck them speechless. Its doorways were embellished with figures molded in stucco. The temple's upper façade reflected a maze of florid designs, and crowning the roof was an elongated "comb" of carved stone. "No description and no drawing can give the moral sublimity of the spectacle," commented Stephens on first viewing the superbly wrought building which was later designated as the Temple of the Inscriptions. And buried deep within the pyramid on which it rested was one of the most startling discoveries in the annals of American archaeology: a century was to pass before the delvings of skilled researchers would bring it to light.

Elsewhere lay still more evidence of Palenque's former grandeur: another temple containing a magnificent altar and delicately inscribed bas-reliefs, an enormous sculptured idol lying face down in the earth, outcroppings of causeways and bridges which had once linked the city together, and other effaced pyramids rising up to obscurity among the relentless mantle of shadowed foliage.

Imprinted upon the ruins were the same distinctive glyph-like inscriptions as those discovered at Copán. They were painted on the walls of the Palace and carved on sculptured monuments. A wall in the Temple of the Inscriptions was inscribed with several "tablets" consisting of hundreds of the unintelligible figures. Superbly etched, the minute carvings—each that of an imaginative animal or human forms, scroll-like devices and florid designs—covered three sections of the temple's innermost chamber. Stephens immediately recognized the inscriptions as hieroglyphs, "the same as those found at Copán. . . ." On the basis of their similarity, he deduced that "there is room for the belief that the whole of this country was once occupied by the same race, speaking the same language, or at least having the same written characters."

But Stephens was reluctant to venture far afield in theorizing as to the identity of Palenque's vanished builders. Earlier visitors to the ruins, including Antonio del Río, whose report had kindled Stephens' initial interest, had attributed the city to foreign emigrants, either from the Old World or some antediluvian point of origin. Stephens felt there was not sufficient basis for any such positive conclusions. Even the native inhabitants of Palenque, he pointed out, knew absolutely nothing of the city's history. "The whole country for miles around is covered by a dense forest of gigantic trees, with a growth of brush and underwood unknown ... in our own country, and impenetrable in any direction except by cutting a way with a machete. What lies buried in that forest it is impossible to say of my own knowledge; without a guide, we might have gone within a hundred feet of the buildings without discovering one of them."

After almost a month at the site the midmorning skies were blanketed with swollen black clouds that rode in on restless winds and broke upon the jungle with drenching fury. The walls of the buildings dripped with moisture, droves of mosquitoes swarmed in their darkened corridors. Rarely had the explorers slept more than three or four hours a night—then it was with "twinging apprehensions of the snakes and reptiles, lizards and scorpions which infested the ruins." By June they were forced to leave Palenque. They followed the course of the Usumacinta River through Chiapas and the alligator-infested lowlands of Tabasco to a point where its green waters flow into the Bay of Campeche. From there they boarded a steamer bound for Yucatán with the intention of examining another ruined city—that of Uxmal near Merída.

Again the sight which confronted them defied their previous expectations which were now accustomed to the miraculous. Standing exposed upon the grass-covered plain was a long building of graceful proportions—The Palace of the Governors. Its façade was embellished with carved stones carefully fitted into a continuous, intricate pattern of geometric designs, stylistic masks, and human faces. Behind the Palace stood other pyramid-shaped structures and mounds of rubble, their details obscured by decay. At the northern limit of the ancient city was a quadrangle of low, flat-topped buildings enclosing a wide courtyard, their surfaces covered with sculptured stone.

And immediately east of this so-called Nunnery Quadrangle a massive pyramid rose at a sharp forty-five-degree angle from the plain to an impressive height. Fifty-four precipitous steps led to a magnificent temple at its summit known as the House of the Dwarf. There could be little doubt that in the days of its glory Uxmal had also been a center of eminent attainments.

The exploration of Uxmal was short-lived. While sketching among the ruins, Catherwood—long suffering from the ravages of acute malaria—lost consciousness and was carried in delirium to a nearby hacienda.

On the thirty-first day of July, 1840, the ship bearing the explorers steamed into New York Harbor. The two men lost no time in preparing the results of their expedition for publication. Stephens' voluminous account entitled *Incidents of Travel in Central America, Chiapas, and Yucatán* appeared in September of 1841. Its impact was phenomenal!

Historians read with mounting dismay his vivid descriptions of the long-ignored ruins—descriptions amplified by Catherwood's crystal-clear etchings. Hastily they sought ways of defending their collapsing beliefs against this new onslaught of contrary evidence. Whole schools of contention sprang up almost overnight to propagate fanciful theories accounting for the existence of the mysterious cities. Scholars re-examined the accounts of earlier travelers and the narratives of the Conquest for clues obscured by their previous complacency; the images reflected in Catherwood's drawings were compared with those of classical and Oriental cultures for possible similarities; cultists seized upon Stephens' findings as "proof" of their beliefs in lost continents and vanished races. Amid the storm of controversy the ever-curious Stephens with his friend Frederick Catherwood re-embarked for Yucatán.

Six weeks were passed completing their unfinished survey of Uxmal. From there they traveled southward to the previously undiscovered remains of Kabah, then past a majestic, three-storied palace known as Sayil to the ruined city of Labná. March of 1842 found them camped at Chichén Itzá—the most impressive of Yucatán's ancient shrines. This was to be the last ruin visited by the two explorers, whose union had already been responsible for the revelation of so many horizons of conjecture. After six months in the field Catherwood's health was again failing, and Stephens—fortified with new discoveries and impressive evidence to support his convictions—was eager to plunge into the waiting caldron of academic debate.

For almost two years his imagination had feasted upon undreamed-of miracles. Before him flashed recollections of his previous travels among the ruins of Egypt, Persia, Arabia, and Greece—the profound accomplishments of those who had carried the seeds of Western Civilization through the corridors of recorded history, resurrecting them from collapsing epochs and projecting them into the "golden ages" which invariably rose out of each new regression to barbarism. But here— buried deep within the mountain-scarred forests of Middle America—were equally accomplished expressions of creative activity, conceived and nurtured wholly outside the realm of existing knoweldge. Had it come to nothing—this outpouring of physical and intellectual energy? Was this but another portent of mankind's failure to maintain its highest orders of society?

Stephens' explorations had laid the undeniable eloquence of Mayan civilization before the world. It was now the concern of scholars to probe beneath the astonishing reality of those attainments for the facts of how and when they had come about.

CHAPTER 4

Myths and Theory:
The Birth of a Science

THE resistance of academic dogmatism was slow to crack under the weight of Stephens' discoveries. That ruins attributable to advanced civilizations actually existed in Middle America could no longer be seriously challenged. But when the question of their origin arose antiquarians steadfastly retreated to the only acceptable sources of possible inspiration: Egypt, Assyria, India, China—in short, any area of influence which would preclude the suggestion of an indigenous development.

Archaeological deposits underlying pre-Columbian remains in the Western Hemisphere were still unprobed, and few students of antiquity had wandered far afield in search of material evidence to support their stubbornly propounded beliefs. The earlier accounts of Del Río, Kingsborough, and Waldeck—which were based almost entirely upon the interpretation of visible remains—did little more than reflect the generally accepted opinion that civilized attainments in the Americas were wrought by peoples other than Indians. The full significance of William Prescott's monumental history of the Spanish Conquest, published in 1832, had not yet been widely recognized. And Bishop Landa's manuscript, *Relación de las cosas de Yucatán,* lay undiscovered in the archives of the Spanish Royal Academy along with numerous other post-Conquest documents which, for all practical purposes, were lost in European libraries. As for existing chronicles, it was generally agreed that the conquistadors had been blinded by their illusions: the ancient cities through which they reportedly passed, the Indian armies they battled, and the treasures they had claimed could not conceivably have been so grand as described.

Stephens had no more insight into the archaeological background of the ruined cities he had explored than did the recognized historians of his day. Yet he wrote with undeniable skepticism of the widely accepted beliefs by which they sought to explain the presence of aboriginal cultures in the Western Hemisphere:

"Volumes without number have been written to account for the first peopling of the Americas. By some, the inhabitants of these continents have been regarded as a separate race. . . . Others have considered them the most ancient race of people upon the earth, ascribing their origin to some remnant of the antediluvian inhabitants of the earth who survived the deluge which swept away the greatest part of the human species in the days of Noah. Under the broad range allowed by a descent from these sons of Noah, many peoples have had ascribed to them the honor of peopling the Americas: the Jews, the Canaanites, the Phoenicians, the Carthaginians, the Greeks, and the Scythians in ancient times; the Chinese, the Swedes, the Norwegians, the Welsh, and the Spaniards in modern times. North and South America have been joined together and rent asunder by the shock of an earthquake; the fabled island of Atlantis has been lifted out of the ocean; and, not to be left behind, an enterprising American has turned the tables on the Old World and planted the ark itself within the state of New York."

Soon the long-dead cities of Middle America became the focal point of an academic controversy seldom if ever surpassed in scope and intensity. So, too, did the less impressive but equally mysterious vestiges of ancient inhabitation scattered across the

United States touch off all manner of spurious theories. "Wild and wandering ideas," Stephens wrote, ". . . have been inspired by the opening of forests, the discovery of tumuli, or mounds, and fortifications extending in ranges from the lakes through the valleys of the Ohio and Mississippi, the finding of mummies in a cave in Kentucky, the discovery on a rock at Dighton of an inscription supposed to be in Phoenician characters, and the unearthing of ruins of walls and a great city in Arkansas and Wisconsin. . . . From such evidence there arose a strong belief that powerful and populous nations had once occupied the country and had passed away, leaving little knowledge of their histories."

But who were the progenitors of these forgotten nations? Where had they come from originally? And what of their eventual destiny? Such speculations—profound enough on the surface—encompassed still broader areas of violent disagreement: biblical interpretation which sought to identify the American Indians with the apocryphal lost Tribes of Israel or survivors of the Deluge; evolution—Darwin's controversial and often misinterpreted hypothesis—seized upon by some as proof that humans in the New World had evolved independently out of extinct varieties of anthropoids; occultism whose advocates insisted upon establishing a "lost continent" as the point of origin of American aborigines.

The result of these conflicting theories was one of unending debate which raged back and forth between historians, theologians, and cultists without hope of resolution. The investigations of Stephens and Catherwood constituted one of the few sobering influences injected into the increasingly violent controversy. Another notable exception was the research carried out by the Abbé Brasseur de Bourbourg, whose delvings in various archives in Europe, Mexico, and Central America turned up numerous forgotten documents bearing upon pre-Columbian civilizations. It was the Abbé Bourbourg who discovered Landa's history of Yucatán in the library of the Spanish Royal Academy in 1863.

Generally speaking, however, the intellectual climate of the nineteenth century was not yet receptive to soundly based scientific conjecture. American archaeology was still the concern of inflexible academicians and deluded mystics working without the benefit of systematic field techniques or correlated methods of research.

It was not unnatural that a dilemma of such protean aspect —that of unaccounted-for races and vanished civilizations— provided rich material for the divinations of cultists and a receptive background for their beliefs in lost continents. Exactly which of the several vanished lands advocated by various occult sects had actually spawned the New World's civilizations became a point of heated disagreement; but there were three persistent choices—Atlantis, the oldest of the mythical continents, Lemuria, and Mu.

Atlantis—whose fame has outlasted all others—had its origin some four centuries before the Christian Era in the fertile imagination of the Greek philosopher Plato. According to Plato's account, this body of land lay just outside the Straits of Gibraltar—"to the west of . . . the Pillars of Hercules," and "was the heart of a great and wonderful empire. . . ." Dominating his imaginary Mecca was a single magnificent city surrounded by a network of canals which led to the ocean. Its principal building was a lavish temple dedicated to the god Poseidon, the supreme ruler of Atlantis, "which remained inaccessible, and was surrounded by an enclosure of gold. . . . The outside of the temple, with the exception of the pinnacles, they covered with silver, and the pinnacles with gold. . . . In the interior . . . the roof was of ivory, adorned everywhere with gold and silver and orichalcum [a metal unknown to the present day]; all the other parts of the walls and pillars and floor they lined with orichalcum. In the

temple they placed statues of gold: there was the god himself
standing in a chariot—the charioteer of six winged horses—
and of such a size that he touched the roof of the building
with his head; around him there were a hundred Nereids riding on dolphins. . . . And around the temple on the outside
were placed statues of gold . . . and other great offerings, both
of kings and private individuals, coming from the city itself
and the foreign cities over which they held sway . . . and there
were [other] palaces in like manner which answered to the
greatness of the kingdom and the glory of the temple."

Beyond this fairytale city the land itself supported a veri-
table paradise: "There was an abundance of wood for car-
penters' work, and sufficient maintenance for tame and wild
animals. Moreover, there were a great number of elephants
. . . and there was provision for animals of every kind, both
for those which live in lakes and marshes and rivers, and for
those which live in mountains and on plains. . . . Also, whatever fragrant things there are in the earth, whether roots, or
herbage, or woods, or distilling drops of flowers and fruits,
grew and thrived . . . and the fruits having hard rind, affording
drinks, and meats, and ointments, and a good store of chest-
nuts . . . all these that sacred island lying beneath the sun
brought forth fair and wondrous in infinite abundance."

We are told that the inhabitants of Atlantis enjoyed this
eternal prosperity "as long as the divine nature lasted in them,
they were obedient to the laws, and well affectioned toward the
gods. . . ." But as invariably happens when humans achieve an
idyllic state, the Atlantians grew fat with greed. "Mortal
admixture" weakened their virtue, the splendor of their existence led to internal decay and the gods ruled that Atlantis
should be destroyed. Accordingly the great floating island was
plunged beneath the sea, never to be heard from again—or so
Plato thought. He had created Atlantis to prove a philo-

sophical point; yet his myth was to become the inspiration for a controversy far removed from its original purpose.

As late as the seventeenth century the fascination of lost continents had influenced no less a proponent of scientific thought than Sir Francis Bacon. In a lengthy treatise entitled *The New Atlantis*, he sought to establish America as the long-vanished continent described by Plato. His narrative recounts a fictitious journey to an island in the newly discovered lands, but it soon becomes apparent that the description of its inhabitants—their laws, traditions, and mode of life—was nothing more than an expression of Bacon's own philosophic Utopia.

Yet the myth of Atlantis persisted as such until 1882 when one Ignatius Donnelly published a book entitled *Atlantis—The Antediluvian World,* and the Greek philosopher's harmless tale became to many a fierce religion. Donnelly attempted to demonstrate "several distinct and novel propositions." He was convinced that the vanished island had once existed "in the Atlantic Ocean, opposite the mouth of the Mediterranean Sea" and that Plato's description of Atlantis was historical fact as opposed to an allegorical fancy. He further maintained that the transition from barbarism to civilization had taken place on Atlantis; and "it became, in the course of ages, a populous and mighty nation, from whose overflowings the shores of the Gulf of Mexico, the Mississippi River, the Amazon, the Pacific coast of South America, the Mediterranean, the west coast of Europe and Africa, the Baltic, the Black Sea and the Caspian were populated by civilized nations."

Carrying his speculations considerably farther than his revered predecessors, Donnelly proposed among other things that "the gods and goddesses of the ancient Greeks, the Phoenicians, the Hindus, and the Scandinavians were simply the kings, queens, and heroes of Atlantis...." He identified

Egypt as "the oldest colony formed by the Atlanteans..."
and set out to prove that the Phoenician alphabet was derived
from Atlantis and disseminated to Europe and Central America; that the mysterious island had been the "seat of the Aryan
or Indo-European family of nations, as well as of the Semitic
peoples, and possibly also the Tauranian races"; and that the
disturbance that submerged the island was actually the biblical
Flood or Deluge.

"If these propositions can be proved," he wrote, "they will
... confirm in many respects the statements in the opening
chapters of Genesis; they will widen the area of human history;
they will explain the remarkable resemblances which exist
between the ancient civilizations found upon the opposite
shores of the Atlantic Ocean ... and they will aid us to re-
habilitate the fathers of our civilization, our blood, and our
fundamental ideas...."

Almost on the heels of Donnelly's work a French student
of antiquities—Augustus Le Plongeon—published a book
based on his travels in Central America and his "excavations"
at Chichén Itzá in Yucatán. Its weighty title, *Sacred Mysteries
Among the Mayas and the Quichés—Their Relation to the
Mysteries of Egypt, Greece, Chaldea and India,* clearly stated
Le Plongeon's conviction: the Maya, along with the ancient
civilizations of Europe and Asia, has evolved from the same
source of inspiration—Atlantis. In this belief, Le Plongeon
spoke for the majority of his occult partisans.

Yet another mythical paradise was said to have existed in
the Indian Ocean. It was known to its adherents as Lemuria
and was supposedly occupied by monsters of the most bizarre
description which gave rise to the primal races of mankind. A
third, more widely discussed vanished island was that of Mu
which extended from the East Indies to the Hawaiian Islands,
and was populated simultaneously by dinosaurs and super-
humans who eventually made their way to the Americas. Once

in popular vogue, the idea of a lost continent implanted itself
firmly in the path of a scholarly solution to the problem of the
ancestry of the American Indian.

Copán

By the turn of the century antiquarians were still groping
for an acceptable answer to the question of human origins in
the Western Hemisphere. Some writers had gone so far as to
relate the Indians to Europeans who migrated to these shores
by way of Iceland and Greenland; others proclaimed them
direct descendants of the Norsemen and Vikings. But as the
panorama of aboriginal cultures continued to unfold, scholars
whose curiosity was not quelled by flights of fancy were beginning to reappraise the problems of American archaeology.

At the conclusion of his investigations, John Lloyd Stephens
insisted that the ruins he had brought to light were those of a
great indigenous civilization—accomplishments born of inherent genius apart from the influence of any other known area
of similar attainments.

Categorically, Stephens ruled out the principal foreign
sources from which the inspiration of Mayan civilization might
have sprung. "I set out with the proposition that they are not
Cyclopean," he wrote, "and do not resemble the works of
Greek or Roman; there is nothing in Europe like them. . . ."
So far as Asia was concerned, Stephens again found little
ground for serious comparison. He emphasized the complete

absence in Middle America of artificially excavated caves and
rock chambers which typified ancient Hindu architecture. Nor
did he concede more than a superficial resemblance between
Hindu sculpture and that produced by the builders of Copán
and Palenque.

Egypt presented a more complex field for speculation. Much
significance had been attributed to the fact that the construction
of pyramids was peculiar to both Egypt and Middle America,
a point which implied to many students a positive cultural link.
Stephens' opposition to this assumption was based on several
factors: "The pyramidal form," he wrote, "is one which suggests itself to human intelligence in every country as the sim-
plest and surest mode of erecting a high structure upon a solid
foundation. It cannot be regarded as a ground for assigning
a common origin to all people among whom structures of that
character are found unless the similarity is preserved in its
most striking features." Egyptian pyramids, he pointed out,
were characteristically uniform in exterior design and were
intended solely as places of burial. American pyramids varied
greatly in form and decorative embellishment and were constructed to elevate and support temples or shrines on their
summits.

With regard to other types of structures, Stephens observed
that columns, "a distinguishing feature of Egyptian architecture," were not evidenced in the ruins he had explored; nor
were the *dromi,* the long avenues of approach, or the *pronaoi*
—porches or vestibules of Egyptian temples. Also there were
marked differences in comparative methods of construction,
and the small stones used to build Copán and its related cities
were, in his words, scarcely "worthy of being laid in the walls
of an Egyptian temple."

Stephens also insisted that more validity be given to the
chronicles of the Conquest—those of Herrera, Bernal Díaz,
and others who had experienced actual contact with the natives

of Middle America. He read with close attention to detail their descriptions of the cities encountered by invading Spanish armies and found them believable by comparison to his own observations. Lastly, the reproductions of hieroglyphic inscriptions published by Lord Kingsborough—principally those contained in the Dresden Codex—were undeniably familiar to Stephens. "We are strongly of the opinion," he stated, "that the characters are the same as those found on the monuments and tablets at Copán and Palenque."

In the light of his investigations, Stephens carefully evaluated the tenets around which the academic controversy of his day revolved. Exploding as it did in a sea of contrary opinion, his answer to the enigma of origins was as daring as it was prophetic. Emphatically he refuted the assumption—so long in vogue—that the aboriginal civilizations of the New World were linked to those of Europe or Asia. "The works of these people," he wrote, "are different from the works of any other known people; they are of a new order, and entirely and absolutely anomalous: they stand alone."

Elsewhere Stephens concluded:

> I am inclined to think that there are not sufficient grounds for the belief in the great antiquity that has been ascribed to these ruins; that they are not the works of people who have passed away and whose history has become unknown. Opposed as is my idea to all previous speculation, I am inclined to think that they were constructed by the races who occupied the country at the time of the invasion by the Spaniards, or by some not very distant progenitors. And I would remark that we began our exploration without any theory to support; our feelings were in favor of going back to a high and venerable antiquity. During the greater part of our journey we were groping in the dark, in doubt and uncertainty, and it was not until our arrival at Uxmal that we formed our opinion of their comparatively modern date. Some are beyond doubt older than others, some are

known to have been inhabited at the time of the Spanish conquest, and others, perhaps, were really in ruins before; and there are points of difference which as yet cannot very readily be explained. But in regard to Uxmal, at least, . . . its desolation and ruin since are easily accounted for. With the arrival of the Spaniards the scepter of the Indians departed. In the city of Mexico every house was razed to the ground, and, beyond doubt, throughout the country every gathering place or stronghold was broken up, the communities scattered, their lofty temples thrown down and their idols burned, the palaces of the caciques ruined, the caciques themselves made bondmen, and, by the same ruthless policy which from time immemorial has been pursued in a conquered country, all the momentos of their ancestors and lost independence were destroyed or made odious in their eyes.

It perhaps destroys much of the interest that hangs over these ruins to assign to them a modern date; but we live in an age whose spirit is to discard phantasms and arrive at truth, and the interest lost in one particular is supplied in another scarcely inferior; for the nearer we can bring the builders of these cities to our own times, the greater is our chance of knowing all. Throughout the country the convents are rich in manuscripts and documents written by the early fathers, caciques, and Indians, who very soon acquired the knowledge of Spanish and the art of writing. These have never been examined with the slightest reference to this subject; and I cannot help thinking that some precious memorial is now mouldering in the library of a neighboring convent which would determine the history of some of these ruined cities; moreover I cannot help believing that the tablets of hieroglyphics will yet be read. No strong curiosity has hitherto been directed to them. . . . For centuries the hieroglyphics of Egypt were inscrutable, and, though not perhaps in our day, I feel persuaded that a key surer than that of the Rosetta Stone will be discovered. And if only three centuries have elapsed since any one of the unknown cities was inhabited, the race of the inhabitants is not extinct. Their descendants are still in

the land, scattered, perhaps, and retired, like our own
Indians, into wildernesses which have not yet been penetrated by a white man. . . .

Thus fifty years before archaeology began to clear away
the debris of reckless theories, Stephens had broken through
the shroud of mystery surrounding the ancient Maya and discerned faint horizons of logic!

Copán

In 1881 an English scholar named Alfred Maudslay embarked upon a series of explorations which signaled the birth
of Mayan archaeology as a science. For thirteen years he
probed the Central American jungles pursuing questions of
practical importance. Where had been the exact geographical
boundaries of Mayan civilization? What evidence was there of
peripheral contact between the Mayan and other pre-Columbian cultures? And were there indications here as elsewhere
throughout the ancient world of history's anomalous cycle—
that of a sudden brilliant florescence which faded slowly into
decline and was reborn in a renaissance standing momentarily
between its fleeting eloquence and collapse. . . .

Maudslay was as energetic as he was inquisitive. He traveled
through vast areas of the countryside, recording and mapping
numerous undiscovered ruins. He made plaster casts of stone

sculpture and applied for the first time the infant art of photography in documenting his findings. Painstakingly he copied hieroglyphic inscriptions in order to compare them with existing codices. At last investigators had at their disposal a definitive summary of factual evidence as opposed to careless speculation, a framework upon which to base a methodical program of research.

In 1892 Harvard University inaugurated a series of expeditions to Middle America largely under the direction of a German explorer-photographer named Teobert Maler. His efforts provided a wealth of information concerning previously unknown regions, especially in the lower Yucatán Peninsula and the Usumacinta Valley. Twenty years later the rapidly advancing field of Mayan studies received another fortunate stimulus: the Carnegie Institution of Washington assigned a permanent staff of specialists to the multiple problems of Middle American research. Under their astute direction, numerous expeditions went forth concerned with specific projects of importance to an over-all understanding of Mayan history. And from the individual undertakings of various other institutions, here and abroad, have come significant contributions toward this goal.

At last the missing dimension was added to the search—actual excavations were begun. Shovels broke the seal of time and penetrated the silent realm of earth and rubble. Certain groups of investigators concentrated their efforts on tracing the evolution of architecture and stone sculpture. Carefully they noted subtle variations in methods and concepts that hinted of early experimentation, outside influences, and established traditions associated with definite periods in Mayan chronology. Others sought to classify the tens of thousands of pottery fragments, which in the hands of trained archaeologists reveal an enormous amount of obscure information. Associations were defined between certain types of pottery and specific chronological periods and geographical locations. Routes of trade and cultural exchange between one city or area and another were gradually evidenced by a careful analysis of the pottery recovered from various ruins.

Still other scholars labored at the singularly important task of deciphering and correlating the divisions of the Mayan calendar with those of our own—to arrive at the means by which the date inscriptions brought to light by excavations could be accurately recorded in terms of Christian chronology. To the Maya, the passing of time was of profound importance. It became an obsession around which their daily lives as well as the broader aspects of their civilization had revolved. They were, in fact, relentlessly beholden to their calendar. No comprehension of Mayan history, philosophy, or religion would be possible without some clue to their calendrical computations; even their architecture was linked to astronomy. In the science of time the Maya far outdistanced every other civilization of the ancient world.

But how to break through the centuries-long silence of Mayan calendrics and interpret their cryptic records? It was a consideration of utmost significance to future research. While Bishop Landa had failed in his attempt to formulate a workable alphabet, he had taken copious notes pertaining to the structure of the Mayan calendar. He learned that certain glyphic representations denoted specific intervals of time—a day, month, year, or one of several larger calendric cycles, and every such hieroglyphic designation was accompanied by numeric devices which denoted the number of these interrelated cycles elapsed since the inception of recorded time. This much Landa was able to glean from his interpreters, but the matter went no further.

In 1887 a German scholar named Ernst Förstemann revived Landa's observations and applied them to inscriptions contained in the Dresden Codex—one of the three surviving Mayan books—with far-reaching results. He worked out the sequence of the interlocking cycles, the order in which they were intended to be read, and made considerable strides toward reducing them to equivalent Gregorian dates. Almost simultaneously an American epigrapher, J. T. Goodman, arrived at similar conclusions which, in effect, corroborated Förstemann's disclosures. The problem was far from resolved at that early date, but it was a beginning on which other scholars were able to elaborate until the astronomical inscriptions could ultimately be read without difficulty. It was perhaps the most important single achievement on which Mayan research would depend.

The actual correlation of Mayan and Gregorian dates has never been fully agreed upon. Efforts to arrive at a positive system have rested largely upon the cross-checking of events recorded in hieroglyphic texts with those to which post-Conquest documents have attributed a precise Gregorian date. By working back from these historically recent starting points, the succession of certain dates inscribed by the Maya could be reconstructed alongside the European time scale. Occasionally, discoveries were made which appeared to offer archaeological confirmation of this parallel chronology. For instance, there are indications that certain astronomical phenomena may have been observed and recorded both in Europe and Middle America, and the dates of these occurrences recorded in their respective calendrical media. Realizing the potential value of bringing these independently recorded dates to bear upon factual events, some scholars sought to utilize such data in establishing a precise chronology. Indeed information of this kind would seem to provide an indisputable point of reference, but other epigraphers have found questionable factors in these calculations and retreated to more reliable historical references contained in both native and Spanish manuscripts. Yet differences of opinion have arisen over certain important factors even in this line of inquiry, with the result that the question of a universally acceptable method of correlation is presently unresolved.

Of the two systems now employed in determining the relative placement of Mayan and Gregorian dates, one was devised by Herbert J. Spinden; another was worked out by J. T. Goodman, Martinez Hernandez, and J. Eric Thompson. While the latter, which has received wide acceptance in recent years, was used as the basis for the dates in this book, it must be noted that new emphasis has recently been afforded Spinden's correlation by the application of radioactive-carbon techniques of dating.

Shortly after the advent of atomic research, it was discovered that the atmosphere contains, among its other elements, particles of radioactive carbon designated as Carbon 14. It is stored within all living organisms in amounts proportionate to the quantity of Carbon 14 in the air. Immediately upon death this natural balance is interrupted and the Carbon 14 retained in the dead organism disintegrates at a given rate. By comparing the amount of radioactive carbon remaining in the decayed matter when it is unearthed with its original ratio, the span of time from the date of death until the remains are examined can be calculated with reasonable accuracy.

Carved wooden lintels excavated at the city of Tikal in north central Guatemala were demonstrated by this method to fall almost exactly within the period ascribed for them by the Spinden chronology. Thus it might well be that further research will force a backward revision in time to the point of greater antiquity which Spinden has steadfastly defended; his dates occur two hundred and sixty years earlier than those of the Goodman-Hernández-Thompson correlation.

Sciences of varied concern were also being applied to Mayan research. Ethnologists launched upon studies of the Indians inhabiting the highlands and rain forests of Middle America— the impoverished survivors of the Conquest—whose physical appearance, folklore, and language still evidence tangible links with the past. Geologists studied the terrain, biologists the wild life and flora in order to outline the effect of environment upon the development of Mayan civilization. The translation and evaluation of historical documents and codices constituted a field of research in itself, one of particular importance where correlations could be gleaned between these sources and the material findings of archaeologists. And the lore of the vanished Maya made its way into literature where it found expression in a number of romantic accounts by adventurers and scientists alike, enamored by the labyrinthine mysteries of a lost civilization.

In his book, *The Origin and History of the Mayas,* M. Wells Jakeman remarks: "A successful reconstruction of Mayan history will . . . afford an unusual opportunity for establishing world parallelisms. The evolution of the Mayan civilization in apparently complete independence of the great culture-complexes of the Old World suggests that its separate historical reconstruction may reveal confirmatory parallels for fixing the chief causes underlying the rise and fall of nations, and for determining the laws of human progress."

A great deal that was not yet known separated scholars from any such pertinent knowledge. As Dr. Jakeman reminds us, it was still not certain exactly who the Maya themselves were, nor had it been disclosed when they arrived in Middle America, or how long they had flourished there. Of particular interest was the baffling paradox of how Mayan culture had flowered in a climatic environment wholly unfavorable to creative endeavors. Even today the torrential rainfall of the Central American lowlands, the enervating heat and rampant disease, discourage all but the most seasoned travelers. Yet the Maya labored for centuries to establish and maintain an empire in the heart of these inhospitable jungles.

And how, Jakeman asks, had the Maya managed to usher in their master civilization almost fully matured from the dawn of its existence? Where was the evidence of feeble beginnings of architecture and sculpture, the infant conceptions out of which grew more advanced inventions in astronomy and mathematics; the crude charts from which sprang their multidivisioned calendar capable of recording millions of years of past or future time? And where were the simple tracings which guided priests toward the invention of hieroglyphic writing? Practically no evidence had been found pointing to any such gradual development in these fields antecedent to their highest florescence. Mayan civilization appeared to have emerged measurably accomplished from its nebulous well of inspiration.

To archaeologists facing questions as enigmatic, as profound, and as seemingly insoluble as these, the search for a beginning along any avenue of approach held only the slightest hope of success. For that matter, Mayan archaeology represented but a single area of study amid dozens laid bare by increasingly active research. Two vast continents, whose faces had teemed with prehistoric life in every conceivable stage of advancement, lay totally unexplored. Systems of government, traditions of art, concepts of religion, in short, an immense storehouse of human knowledge, awaited the probing of men concerned with extricating the lessons of the past. The interrelationship of history had long before been established, and here was an incredibly rich field for comparative study. The origin of the Indian and the inspiration of advanced civilizations in the Americas were still shrouded in the deepest of archaeological mystery. Here and there, however, the veil of darkness was giving way before the inquiry of scholars; the element of chance discovery now resided in their camp.

CHAPTER 5

The American Indian:
The Problem of Origins

ACCIDENTAL discovery has been called the handmaiden of archaeological progress. Seldom have scientists taken a specific problem into the field with the assurance that the often laborious task of excavating a predetermined site will produce its solution. Usually it works in reverse—a chance discovery by inquisitive laymen lays bare a route of inquiry for archaeologists to follow. So it was when an accidental "find" provided the first break in what had long been the enigma of man's lineage in the Western Hemisphere.

For many years students had been intrigued by a curious type of flint projectile point found at various locations in the western half of the United States. These so-called "fluted points" varied somewhat in size and shape, but all had one peculiar feature in common: they were thin and finely wrought with a deep longitudinal groove extending from their base almost to the tip along each face of the blade.

In 1926 one such point found near the town of Folsom, New Mexico, came to the attention of archaeologists at the Denver Museum of Natural History. It had reportedly been uncovered in direct association with animal bones of seemingly great antiquity. Suspecting that the discovery might be of considerably greater significance than was at first apparent, a group of specialists representing various scientific institutions journeyed to Folsom to examine the site more closely. Immediately they set to work uncovering and reconstructing what had taken place there on the arid plain centuries before. Numbers of the disarticulated skeletons were unearthed, together with still more of the peculiar fluted blades. The bones were those of a species of bison—heavy-horned creatures which had once roamed about in large herds just as their more recent cousins, the American buffalo, had until a century ago. But what touched off a flurry of excited speculation was the fact that this particular type of bison had not grazed on those plains for perhaps ten or fifteen thousand years! Here, then, were man-made implements associated with the bones of long-extinct animals. One of the curiously shaped points was found imbedded between the crumbling ribs of its prey—positive proof that humans had tracked down and slaughtered the beasts at that very place possibly ten thousand years before.

Every fragment of evidence from the Folsom site was carefully collected and examined by a jury of specialists. There could be no question that what they had uncovered was just such a graveyard left behind by prehistoric hunters. What only a few months before had been a meaningless pile of weathered bones eroding from a dry arroyo had become an archaeological treasure. Our knowledge of man's age in the New World had been immeasurably enriched. It was now certain that humans—perhaps the direct forebears of the American Indians—had lived and hunted on this continent for at least ten thousand years.

A time factor of such magnitude had far-reaching results. It established the fact that human history had begun in this hemisphere at an earlier date than was previously supposed by most serious students; prior to the Folsom discovery few anthropologists would have conceded that men had subsisted in the Americas on the flesh of long-extinct animals. With the evidence now at hand, scholars were able to turn the scientific tide against the propagation of unsound speculations as to the origin of the New World's aboriginal inhabitants. If, as it had been proclaimed, they were descended from some super-civilization, how were findings which argued conclusively for a level of incipient culture in this hemisphere comparable to Paleolithic or Stone Age remains in Europe and Asia to be explained? Such evidence indicated a gradual progression in human development rather than a sudden brilliant entrance onto the stage of civilized attainment.

From a second discovery of startling aspect came further confirmation that rudely cultured tribesmen had stalked these environs at a date far earlier even than the Folsom hunters. High in the Sandia Mountains overlooking Albuquerque, New Mexico, a cave was discovered in 1937 which attracted the interest of archaeologists from the University of New Mexico.

Bearing in mind the archaeological law that the oldest debris invariably lies at the bottom of the heap, excavators under the direction of Frank C. Hibben—a specialist in the field of early man—began digging into the cave's subsurface deposits. Below the upper layer of historically recent artifacts they unearthed Folsom points mixed with charred animal bones and charcoal from ancient campfires. Digging still lower under this accumulation of Folsom material, they encountered a deposit of sterile yellow ocher. Beneath the ocher was still another level of human occupation.

Scattered about this lowest horizon of the cave, Hibben found animal bones, charcoal, rough flint scrapers, and knives; but the spearheads from this stratum were totally different from Folsom points. These were roughly oval in shape, crudely chipped, and with an indentation at one side of their base.

The cave's geological stratigraphy clearly indicated that whatever people had fashioned these "Sandia points" had dwelt there considerably earlier than its Folsom occupants, for it requires a prodigious span of time for such well-defined levels —separated by layers of sterile earth—to accumulate. Although it is perfectly logical to assume that the Folsom hunters produced more than one characteristic type of weapon, it did not stand to reason that the same people who turned out the superbly executed grooved points would also have fashioned the crude, badly flaked Sandia points—at least not simultaneously. It was abundantly clear that Sandia Cave had been the scene of two distinct occupations separated by thousands of years.

Aside from the matter of spear points, however, Hibben noted that the remains from the two levels told more or less identical stories. Both the Folsom hunters and their Sandia predecessors had lived in the cavern for a considerable length of time. Into their lair they had dragged the carcasses of slain animals, skinned them, cooked the flesh, and scattered the bones about the floor. Amid this refuse they had eaten, slept, and manufactured the bare necessities of life. When they abandoned their mountain home, the debris left behind was gradually covered over by dust and water-borne deposits until the cave's next inhabitants centuries later were very probably unaware that others had lived there before them. Thus nature itself preserved the sequence of past events. By computing the length of time required for each successive level to amass, archaeologists can often read and interpret the story of human life recorded in the stratified earth and gauge with reasonable accuracy the lapses of time involved. On the basis of such geologic stratigraphy, Hibben estimated that the Sandia Cave's earliest inhabitants had dwelled there perhaps as long ago as twenty thousand years!

Elsewhere other caverns have yielded human debris associated with the remains of extinct animals, though not as ancient as the Sandia discovery. A site in Nevada known as Gypsum Cave was found to contain man-made implements and charcoal

along with bones of horses, camels, and sloths estimated by
Carbon 14 tests to be between eight and ten thousand years in
age. Similar findings have occurred in Arizona, Utah, and as
far east as Alabama where a deep rock shelter called Russell
Cave has produced evidence of a continuous occupation reaching back some nine thousand years. Quite recently sites near
Tule Springs, Nevada, Santa Rosa Island, California, and
Lewisville, Texas, have yielded radiocarbon dates which indicate human activity in the Americas may have begun as far back
as thirty thousand years and probably much earlier.

What has been gleaned so far about the appearance, material
culture, and mode of life of these first inhabitants of the New
World is a creditable example of archaeological deduction.
Remembering that the obscure record of events has been
gleaned from extremely fragmentary evidence—based primarily upon the association of man-made implements with
bones of extinct animals—it is hardly surprising that much remains to be learned. Yet a reasonably sound basis for speculation can be inferred from a comparative study of the findings to
date.

Undoubtedly, this hemisphere's earliest inhabitants ordered
their lives by the necessity to hunt. Occasionally their diet
of semi-raw flesh was supplemented with nuts, berries, and
grain gathered from food-bearing plants, although true agriculture was wholly unknown to them. Hunting and gathering
are a precarious basis for existence; they necessitate moving
about endlessly from one place to another in search of unde-
pleted herds and virgin woodlands.

Apparently these nomadic peoples did so with agility and
skill. Numbers of Folsom points have been found along the
fringes of the Rocky Mountains. Near Lindenmeir in Colorado
an extensive camp site was discovered where these hunters had
not only killed quantities of extinct animals, but had cooked
the flesh over open fires and apparently dressed the skins with

crude stone scrapers. Dry arroyos and sand pits on the out-skirts of Clovis, New Mexico, yielded evidence that other groups, perhaps distinct from the Folsom nomads, had hunted and dwelled in the vicinity for a long period of time. Unmistakable signs of the wanderings and hunting prowess of the first Americans have come to light in at least a dozen other widely scattered sites in the western and middle United States.

From all indications they were masters of the hunting methods dictated by their weapons and the habits of their prey. They were without the bow and arrow—the device so closely associated with the American Indians. It was a later innovation, far later than the remote span of time that encompassed the scene of humans slaughtering long-vanished animals which the eyes of historic Indians would never behold. Instead they used a "throwing stick" or *atlatl* that afforded greater power than spears hurled by hand. Once an animal fell wounded under its impact, other spearsmen perhaps rushed from their hiding places to share in the kill by planting their weapons at close range. A curious array of animals—mammoth, giant sloths, miniature horses, saber-toothed cats, bison, and camels—had fallen before their skillfully aimed spears.

Artifacts from the camp sites of early man confirm the simplicity of their existence. Always there are the tools of the hunter—his spear points and crude stone knives—and oval flint blades carefully chipped along one side served as scrapers for dressing skins for use as clothing. Layers of charcoal denote their campfires where the flesh was cooked and eaten. Occasionally bones were sharpened or otherwise altered to form awls or fleshers, and heavier stones were flaked along one edge to serve as choppers or rubbed smooth to use for pounding. It is generally believed that these early nomads possessed domesticated dogs; and there is conclusive evidence that they were skilled at weaving with vegetable fibers—sandals and matting have been uncovered in caves in Utah, Oregon, and Nevada which were shown by Carbon 14 analysis to be of very great antiquity.

When we approach the question of the actual physical appearance of the people with whose material remains we are dealing, anthropologists present us with desultory evidence which is much less positive in its implications. A number of seemingly ancient human skeletal remains have been found, frequently in association with the bones of extinct animals. Such finds have occurred from California to Florida and deep into South America. But the conditions surrounding these discoveries have failed to convince many authorities who examined them that they were of sufficient age to link them with the earliest inhabitants of the American continents. In many instances the important geological deposits containing the remains had been overturned or disturbed, thus destroying the datable stratigraphy. In others the skeletons were believed to be comparatively recent burials interred by chance in more ancient deposits.

Several curious paradoxes occur in the possibly ancient remains studied so far. A group of burials found in the loess beds of Nebraska had skulls which the physical anthropologist Aleš Hrdlička—who was vehemently opposed to the supposition that man in the New World was of great antiquity—was forced to admit were very similar to those of Neanderthal Man in Europe. However, the skeletons themselves were of essentially modern Indian types. In other cases where skulls of "primitive" character were found, the conditions surrounding their discovery did not appear to indicate that they were of very great age. As for two other skeletons for which there is a reasonable probability of an antiquity of perhaps fifteen thousand years, both are modern in appearance. Known ironically as Minnesota Man and Midland (Texas) Man, both skeletons were those of women.

While the question of "primitive" versus "modern" physical

types had a considerable bearing upon earlier calculations as to man's age in the Americas, it is no longer regarded as a primary factor in such speculations. In her excellent summary of these problems, *Ancient Man in North America,* H. M. Wormington points out that the "... firm belief that skeletons more than a few thousand years old must differ markedly from those of more recent times, and must be considerably more primitive, is regarded as unjustified by present-day anthropologists. There is ample evidence that modern types of men were present in the Old World during the late Pleistocene, and North American skeletons need not show particularly archaic features in order to be attributed to that period."

Most authorities agree with this summation: the earliest inhabitants of the Western Hemisphere—who arrived here perhaps as long ago as thirty thousand years—differed very little in appearance from their historic Indian descendants.

Copán

Assuming then—on the strength of the evidence before us—that the Sandia and Folsom hunters were among the first humans to enter this hemisphere, we must still answer the perplexing question of where they came from originally. Indeed this is the very essence of the enigma shrouding man's origin in the New World.

One fact in the amorphous succession of events with which we are dealing is certain: the earliest evidences of human life in the Americas appear toward the end of the geological period known as the Pleistocene, during which the upper half of the earth's surface was periodically enveloped in catastrophic sheets of ice.

On the Euro-Asian continents—against this frigid background—less intelligent and adaptable forms of anthropoid life had slowly emerged from the milieu of cosmic occurrences that nurtured the rise of mankind. In the shadowed depths of Pleistocene time man strode slowly along the path of evolution until he stood erect, hunted with tools of his own making, dressed in skins, and struck fire from flint. His footsteps are marked by the remains of his faltering efforts to apply and improve his dawning abilities: roughly altered stones gave way to skillfully worked implements of flint and finely polished axes; in time the mysteries of his environment inspired him to fashion magic-laden drawings and molded images with which to appease his fear of the unknown. By the end of the Pleistocene, humans—fully developed in appearance, inventive, curious, and keenly in awe of the supernatural—had wandered over all of Europe, Asia, and Africa. Why, during this era of restless migrations, should man not have found his way to America as well? The road was open and tempting.

But where might have been his route of entry into the fertile western continents? Significantly the trail of early man led toward Canada and Alaska. Evidence of extremely ancient inhabitation was disclosed along the Columbia River in Oregon. Folsom- and Sandia-type implements appeared in Alberta and Saskatchewan, and Folsom points were picked up at various places in Alaska, including the barren, rock-strewn coasts of the Bering Strait. This was an especially salient fact. At this point scarcely fifty-six miles of water divide the shores of Alaska and Siberia. Asia and North America almost literally join hands across this inhospitable sea. On the basis of the physical appearance of most Indians—their straight hair, constricted eyes, and predominantly high cheekbones—there had long been reason to look to Asia as the point of origin of their ancestors. Here, then, was a direct link between the East and West which had been overlooked in previous speculations, a possible point of entry through which wandering peoples from Asia could have gained access to the American continents.

Geologists were able to confirm the feasibility of this assumption. They presented impressive evidence to support the belief that the Bering Strait had been easily passable at specific intervals during the last quarter of the Pleistocene. Voluminous amounts of water were drawn up from the seas, held solid in mountainous blue-white glaciers on the land. Once turbulent seas were stilled or weakened by the loss of water; a shallow area such as the Bering Strait was very probably frozen solid or reduced to dry land, thus forming a natural bridge from Asia to America. Across such a bridge the ancestors of the American Indians could have traveled from an already old world into the fertile lands beyond, unaware that they were migrating from one hemisphere to another. Undoubtedly they came as hunters in search of prey, tracking the restless herds of horses, camels, bison, and mammoths across the glacier-locked northlands.

Gradually they moved south in a series of sweeping migrations, which brought them from the Yukon and Mackenzie valleys down through Oregon and Nevada into lower California; another route carried them along the eastern side of the Rocky Mountains. Eventually groups of these nomadic hunters ventured toward the Atlantic coast and penetrated deep into South America. Ecuador and Brazil have yielded human remains associated with extinct animals, and Carbon 14 tests indicated that humans were occupying caves in southern Chile some nine thousand years ago.

Almost certainly there were a series of southward migrations covering an immense span of time; perhaps there was even a continuous interchange of life during the period when the Bering Strait was passable. Anthropologists know of these happenings only in essential outline; much is still clouded by lack of evidence and can only be inferred by fragmentary indications. It is certain, however, that humans were in the New World en masse as the last glaciers retreated from their epochal encroachment upon the earth some fifteen thousand years ago. As the ice diminished and the land gradually warmed, diversified groups of hunting and gathering peoples inherited the American continents. Of the millennia that elapsed between their arrival and the emergence of recognizable Indian tribes, very little has been learned. Exactly what happened during this long interval in American prehistory—the complex exchange of ideas and inventions, the amassing of cultural influences—is not clearly defined by the scattered remains upon which the archaeological reconstruction of these happenings must depend. Ultimately, however, the incipient foundations of tribes came about: a more sedentary mode of existence altered the earlier traditions of hunting and gathering; groups banded together, uniting behind distinct barriers of language, custom, and religious beliefs into autonomous tribes.

It was perhaps five thousand years ago that agriculture first spread its life-giving stimulus among the Indians. Somewhere in the Central or South American highlands tribesmen experimented—by what means we do not know—with the cross-pollination of wild plants and discovered the great staple of life—maize or Indian corn. Once attained, such knowledge spread rapidly northward and led in many directions, until the Indians had developed tomatoes, avocados, beans, melons, squash, cotton, potatoes, cassava, and a dozen other crops which could be cultivated at will. No longer was it necessary to depend upon hunting and gathering; there was time now for less prosaic endeavors.

Agriculture in the New World appears to have developed completely apart from similar advances in Europe and Asia. None of the major food-bearing plants upon which the Indians depended for sustenance were known in the Eastern Hemisphere prior to Columbus. Likewise, the prime staples of Indo-European economy—wheat, barley, and rice—were never grown in pre-Columbian America. It is possible, however, that future archaeological research carried out on a cooperative international scale may yet define highroads over which previously unsuspected influences traveled back and forth between hemispheres. Discoveries such as these might well explain a number of curiously unnatural parallelisms without disrupting the overwhelming certainty that the major achievements of pre-Columbian civilization were basically indigenous in origin.

By the seventh century after Christ, the New World was warmed by the brilliance of a dozen golden ages. In the Andean highlands pre-Incan tribesmen had traversed the sharp-peaked mountains surrounding their prospering cities with a network of highways and bridges that defy the imagination. Added to this were cyclopean feats of construction—tons of granitic stone exactingly cut and elevated to the walls of temples and fortresses, held in place by well-mastered principles of balance and stress. Long before, they had developed ceramics and woven textiles that place among the finest examples of those arts known to the ancient world.

To the north, in Mexico, numbers of ruined cities attest to the eloquence of the elusive civilizers who transmitted the knowledge of sculpture, calendrics, and architecture throughout the central plateau centuries before Cortéz stepped ashore at Veracruz in the spring of 1519.

North of the Rio Grande the continental United States and

Canada had become the dominion of tribal nations less attuned to the civilizing forces of Middle America. Their legacy was not inspired by the transcendent genius of geographically distant Mexico. It was not born of star-sightings, mathematics, engineering, hieroglyphics, and sculpture; nor was it adorned with theocracies, royalty, grand armies, or empires. Never was it synthesized by a community of effort that raised city after city in which to enshrine eternal mysteries, or latticed mountains and labyrinthine jungles with stone-coated highways over which to bear high priests and royal processions.

Rather theirs was a simpler inheritance wrought by the bronze-sinewed hands of hunters who followed game trails through canyon-scarred mountains and across endless plains, where the afterworld of spirits and demons fused closely with images of reality. Here in the northern half of the hemisphere the elements of environment were irascible and harsh, and the secured leisure of agriculture was never enjoyed so fully as in Middle America. Life remained nearer to its elemental components.

Monumental achievements were amassed with the framework of these aboriginal cultures. Approximately one hundred and sixty linguistic stocks containing over twelve hundred dialectic subdivisions gave North and South America more spoken languages than the remainder of the ancient world. Some four hundred major tribal groups—in varying stages of advancement—flourished within fifteen separate culture areas. There is scarcely a square mile of the Americas in which one cannot find traces of pre-Columbian habitation.

Centuries before the Conquest the Indians had cultivated at least twenty important food-bearing plants, more than doubling the world's agricultural potential. They had domesticated the dog—which they probably brought to this continent with them —the turkey, llama, alpaca, ducks, and bees. In the Andes the knowledge of medication and narcotics was well advanced. Ex-

A stela in the Great Plaza, Copan.

All photographs by the author unless otherwise indicated.

The Hieroglyphic Stairway, Copan.

Detail of an altar, Copan.

Detail of Stela H, Copan.

The Ball Court, Copan.

Detail of Stela N, Copan.

Detail of Stela C, Copan.

An example of Maya hieroglyphic writing, Piedras Negras.
(*National Museum of Guatemala*)

Section of Stela 12 showing details of sculpture, Piedras Negras.
(*National Museum of Guatemala*)

Detail of Stela 6, Piedras Negras. (*National Museum of Guatemala*)

The Peten rain forest, Guatemala.

Temple II, Tikal.

Temple III, Tikal.

Temple I, Tikal. Under restoration by the University of Pennsylvania.

A stela standing before circular altars, Tikal.

Back view of Temple V, Tikal. Note hieroglyphic inscriptions covering upper portion.

Sculptural detail of a throne, Piedras Negras. (*National Museum of Guatemala*)

A wall panel excavated at Piedras Negras.
(*National Museum of Guatemala*)

Restoration of the same panel by M. Louise Baker.
(*National Museum of Guatemala*)

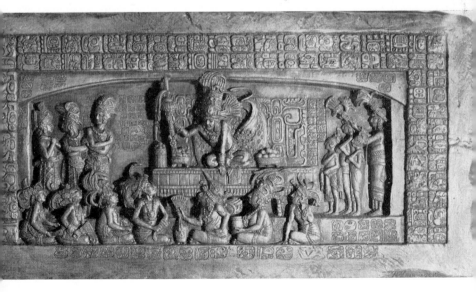

A limestone relief showing the ceremonial offering of a vessel, Jonuta, Tabasco. (*National Museum of Mexico*)

perimentation with surgery was in progress, including the delicate operation of trepanning—removing skull fragments to
relieve cerebral pressure.

Objects of gold, silver, copper, and bronze are encountered
in historically late horizons in Middle America and the Andean
highlands. But metals *never* uprooted the Indians' primary de-
pendence upon stone implements. It was perhaps the turning
point of their history that, once discovered, metals did not
usher in an Iron Age similar to that which revolutionized
Europe in the three thousand years before Christ. The New
World remained in a perennial Age of Stone. Metal came only
in the twilight of its highest civilizations and found few uses
outside of ornamentation. Elsewhere throughout the ancient
world its application to war and the welding of empires had
long been its foremost merit.

A comparable paradox lies in the principle of the wheel.
History had rolled across Europe and Asia in chariots of war
—Egyptian, Assyrian, Greek, and Roman. The catapults of
Moorish invaders and Norman knights, the cannon of Charles
the Fifth, the Hapsburgs, and Napoleon moved on wheels,
which from the moment of their conception became the prime
stimulant to the significant schemes of Indo-European history.
Yet among the New World's civilizers the wheel remained
nothing more than a pathetic experiment. On the Mexican
plateau fragile clay wheels were mounted under toy models of
carts; beyond that there is no evidence of their application to
the myriad problems of empire building.

It is essentially clear that pre-Columbian civilization reached
its apex without the major prerequisites of higher attainments
found everywhere else in antiquity: the smelting of metals, the
principle of the wheel, beasts of burden, the plow, and the potter's wheel. Upon these accruements had ridden the flood of
civilization elsewhere. Yet in view of such shortcomings the

emergence of otherwise advanced cultures becomes all the more incredible.

This, then, in brief outline was the massive panorama of ancient America during the opaque millennia before its discovery and conquest: centuries-long migrations from Asia of men and Ice Age animals across the frozen Bering Strait and southward over the whole of the Western Hemisphere; the complex diffusion of rudely cultured hunters into distinct tribes bound by custom and religion; the giving way of nomadic instincts before the warming flood of agriculture, which brought in its wake the leisure and semi-urbanization that fostered invention, experimentation, and the birth of civilized endeavors. Somewhere among the Ice Age hunters were the ancestors of the Maya—whose innovators were destined to achievements superior to all others who now possessed the fertile Western continents. Out of the New World's dawning cultures the Maya would suddenly surge forward to become what the Greeks had been to the Classic world—purveyors of eminent attainments, guardians of celestial knowledge.

CHAPTER 6

The Search for a Beginning

LYING across the northern portion of Guatemala is a vast expanse of forest-covered lowlands known as El Petén. It is situated roughly in the geographical center of the territory occupied by the Maya at the time their maximum expansion was reached in the ninth century. Its density and unfavorable conditions had defied all but sporadic investigations until 1926 when the Carnegie Institution of Washington began extensive excavations among the ruins of a city located in the heart of the Petén's cavernous depths.

It was named Uaxactún. Its structures lay in formless mounds of rubble scarcely visible under a canopy of mahogany, sapodilla, and ceiba trees thickly enshrouded with vines. Little or no human life existed in the Petén at the time of Uaxactún's discovery. In searching out evidence of former habitation there archaeologists had entered upon unknown ground.

During preliminary explorations in 1916, the noted scholar Sylvanus Morley had reclaimed a deeply eroded stone monument from the ruins of Uaxactún. Later examination revealed that his discovery (designated as Stela 9) recorded in barely discernible glyphs a date equivalent to April 9, A.D. 328. It was the oldest dated monument ever brought to light in the Mayan area. It seemed feasible, therefore, that excavations at Uaxactún might provide the long-sought inroad to the problem of reconstructing the origins of Mayan civilization. It was a possibility worthy of the herculean task required to test its validity; thus far virtually nothing had come into the hands of archaeologists by which they could accurately retrace the developmental steps incident to the growth of Mayan culture.

Some years later a corps of laborers went to work clearing the underbrush from the debris-littered mounds. A cluster of pyramidal ruins designated as Group E were among the remains selected for excavation, and the seventh structure in this series proved to be the key for which archaeologists had been searching. At first appearance the crumbled pyramid was not unlike the majority of others at Uaxactún. It had once risen up in a series of diminishing terraces to a flat summit. As it had been the custom of Mayan builders to add successive layers to their structures at specific intervals of time, a second pyramid in a considerably better state of preservation was soon disclosed underneath the outer shell. This original structure—known as E-VII-sub—was barely twenty-eight feet in height and was ascended by a single flight of broad steps on each of its sides. The stairways were divided by vertical rows of ponderous stone jaguar masks, numbering eighteen in all. It was obvious that stonemasons had not yet achieved full mastery of their materials when the huge heads were fashioned and set into place on the pyramid's terraced slopes; yet conceptions are reflected in their efforts which were perfected and amplified during centuries to come.

Originally the entire surface of pyramid E-VII-sub had been coated with gleaming white plaster. And its construction had predated the later practice of gracing such pyramidal elevations with elaborate stone temples. On its summit, instead, was the outline of what had once been a structure probably of stucco walls and thatched roof on a framework of poles. Obviously the construction of permanent stone buildings had not yet evolved when the E-VII-sub stood in its original splendor, and it had been erected long *before* Stela 9 was set up to commemorate some cryptic happening in the year A.D. 328. It was,

Morley wrote, ". . . the oldest Maya stone construction that has come down to us and probably dates from the second century of the Christian Era." *

Subsequent excavations at Uaxactún were to form a broad foundation on which to base research in future years. For concealed in its ruins was the long-missing key to the processes by which the Maya had emerged from agrarian tribesmen to the bearers of a highly advanced culture.

It was perhaps two thousand years before the Christian Era when the forerunners of the Maya ended their fortuitous wanderings in the tropical heart of Middle America. Almost certainly they were not the first humans to inhabit the region. Nomadic hunters had likely stalked its forests for untold centuries. Ultimately, however, with the advent of agriculture, the Maya were stirred by a new mode of existence which gradually overtook the land, giving rise to a level of culture known as "Archaic"—when a sedentary pattern of life made necessary the establishment of permanent settlements and various cultures began to evolve along divergent routes of expression. It was the dawn in which the outlines of higher attainments were first faintly visible.

Excavations in widely scattered areas have provided a fragmentary reconstruction of the manner of life during this earliest period of continuous occupation. Skillfully executed implements of stone—axes, knives, scrapers, and grinding tools—are found in abundance. Vegetable fibers and cotton were utilized to weave nets, baskets, matting, and fabric. The sole instruments of agriculture were stone-edged hoes and sticks with fire-hardened points for planting seed. Utilitarian pottery bowls and jars were commonly used, occasionally with painted or incised geometric designs or effigy representations. Figurines in the

* Reprinted from *The Ancient Maya*, by Sylvanus G. Morley, with the permission of the publishers, Stanford University Press. Copyright 1946, 1947, and 1956 by the Board of Trustees of Leland Stanford Junior University.

shape of grossly exaggerated female forms, perhaps symbolic of fertility, are frequently unearthed in Archaic sites.

Scattered across thousands of miles of jungle and mountainous plateaus were the loosely knit settlements of these early farming peoples: latticed fields of crops on the edges of which squatted irregular rows of low-roofed thatched dwellings with packed earthen floors. Nearby were clusters of ceremonial structures—uninhabited until a predetermined day of ritual when the enclosures teemed with the populace from miles around. It was a bare existence made all the more exigent by the mysteries of the environment.

Life depended entirely upon the rhythm of seasonal change —upon sun and rain—the uninterrupted sowing and harvesting of crops in amounts ample to support the delicate balance of a newly sedentary economy. Nature alone was the sole material of survival. Her manifestations were deified; appeasing her caprices motivated a ceaseless round of ritual adoration; probing her mysteries became the sanctimonious striving of risingly powerful priesthoods.

Very early in Mayan history the permutations of the heavens were recognized as bearing directly upon the growth of crops, therefore upon sustenance itself. And it was believed that the stars foretold in their wanderings back and forth across the night skies the predestination of man. Mayan priests measured the continuance of life against their ability to chart and interpret these celestial machinations. They began to observe the skies along immovable lines of sight and note the seasonal variations that came with the gradually shifting positions of the stars. Long afterward the length of the tropical and sidereal years was finally determined, along with the span of each lunar cycle—the measure of a single month. Such knowledge became the keystone of their incredibly accurate calendrical system.

Together with these advances in astronomy came the need

for a means of permanently recording calendrical computations
—hence the priests began devising hieroglyphic writing and a
system of numerology. Obscure, indeed, are the precursory
steps that led to these inventions; no record of their preliminary development has been recovered by excavation. It was
suggested that advances preceding the maturity of these innovations may have been recorded on wooden tablets, rawhide
scrolls, or some other highly perishable materials, prior to the
appearance of stone sculpture as a medium of expression.
Whatever the path of their development, calendrics and hieroglyphic writing became the primary factors around which the
later achievements of the Maya were to revolve. With such
knowledge at their command the priesthoods were able to pre-
direct mammoth outpourings of human energy toward specific
endeavors—a prerequisite to the flood of civilized attainment
about to break into a thousand-year dominance over the land.

As the desire to record the passage of time, so closely allied
with religious beliefs, inspired the invention of a written
language and a mathematical system, so, too, was the search
for creative expression through art and architecture concerned
with the formalization of religious ideals. And once devised,
images of aesthetic importance were handed down by the priesthoods—whose influence in such matters was illimitable—to engineers and artisans in whose hands they were indelibly trans-
posed onto buildings and monuments.

Gradually architects learned to construct thick-walled buildings of solid masonry to replace the stucco and thatch structures of earlier centuries. Yet the Maya never discovered the
use of the true arch; instead they conceived a corbeled arch
which required a ceiling steeply vaulted toward a central cap
stone, causing the buildings to appear peculiarly top-heavy owing to the volume of masonry necessary to distribute the roof's
weight.

Along with the introduction of corbeled vaulted buildings

there began the curious practice of erecting date-markers or
stelae to commemorate specific intervals of time. These were
the ornately carved shafts of stone which Stephens had tenta-
tively referred to as "idols." Fortunately for archaeological
research, the Maya set them up with obsessive regularity at
intervals predetermined by the divisions of their calendar.
Stelae have proved to be the most valuable weapon with which
scholars have attacked the gigantic puzzle of Mayan history,
for they provide a continuous sequence of dates from which to
infer otherwise imperceptible happenings.

Sculptors were assigned the task of inscribing upon stelae the
reckonings of astronomer-priests—artisans inspired by the
necromancy of the heavens and devoted to the perpetuity of
their creations. Working with none but stone implements, they
fashioned in sandstone, dolomite, limestone, and even harder
trachyte the cherished images of deities accompanied by hieroglyphic inscriptions which preserved for posterity the exact
moment at which a new work was consecrated to the gods . . .
a massive pyramid . . . a temple . . . a superbly carved altar of
polished granite. Or perhaps the stelae recorded a calendric
cycle of time coming around again on its ceaseless course, to
receive the homage of those who waited tirelessly for the
portents of the good or bad fortune it would bring.

Thus it was that Mayan "civilization" would seem to have
been launched with the firm mastery of stone architecture em-
ploying vaulted ceilings and hieroglyphic writing applied to the
erection of dated stelae. For the "golden age" of the Maya—
the inception of the so-called Old Empire or Classic period—
appears to have begun with the gradual spread of these elements which, in turn, presaged the founding of ceremonial centers. Bound as were these purely mechanical advances to the
religious nature of the Maya, they became the cornerstone of
their cultural development. Architecture and sculpture allowed
the permanent enshrinement of their ideals; hieroglyphic stelae

recorded their devotion to the mysteries of time for reasons we shall soon examine. With such knowledge at hand the upsurge toward a Golden Age was begun!

Piedras Negras

But where had these unique manifestations been born? Where, indeed, did the nucleus of Mayan ingenuity first emerge from its obscure background? Uaxactún provided a significant clue.

Excavations revealed that vaulted architecture, superbly executed pottery (an ornate polychrome ware found abundantly in Classic sites), and hieroglyphic monuments whose date inscriptions reached back farther into time than any previously uncovered were present at Uaxactún by the middle of the fourth century. Furthermore, the erection in still more ancient times of pyramid E-VII-sub—which represented perhaps the earliest step in the evolution of Mayan architecture found thus far—left little doubt that Uaxactún had flowered at the very dawn of Mayan emergence as a distinct civilization. It was further disclosed that succeeding advances in these fields—improvements in design and workmanship—could be correlated with specific periods of time. Especially was this true in the case of the pottery recovered from Uaxactún, and once such relationships were defined their application to other archaeological sites made possible parallel reconstructions in the spread of Mayan culture over a large geographical area.

Accordingly Uaxactún was recognized as one of the first

cities to have witnessed the birth of higher attainments, thus it now seemed reasonable to assume as well that the vicinity of the Petén forests had been the background against which the Maya underwent the monumental transition from blindly groping tribesmen to the bearers of a superbly accomplished culture.

But Uaxactún was certainly not the only center of activity during these formative centuries. In 1864 a jade pendant—the Leyden Plate—was found on the outskirts of Puerto Barrios in Guatemala. It was eight and a half inches long by three inches wide, and its polished surface was inscribed with an ornate human figure in low relief. On the back was a hieroglyphic inscription corresponding to the year A.D. 320, establishing it as slightly more than seven years older than Stela 9 from Uaxactún. Morley has pointed out the unmistakable similarity between the style of carving on the Leyden Plate and inscriptions uncovered at Tikal, an extensive ruin located several miles south of Uaxactún. Such evidence, he concluded, would indicate that Tikal's origins were even more remote in time than Uaxactún's. Recent excavations by the University of Pennsylvania are confirming this possibility; levels of occupation have been uncovered at Tikal which extend far back into pre-Classic horizons.

A still more ancient object known as the "Tuxtla Statuette" was unearthed in Veracruz—a small stone figurine in the form of a duck-billed effigy. It bore a date written in Mayan glyphs equivalent to A.D. 162. But it has not been ascertained whether the Tuxtla figure is of Mayan origin or if it is the work of a people on the periphery of their influence. Here, indeed, lies an interesting field for speculation and future research. Veracruz and Tabasco—areas immediately bordering the former Mayan realm—have yielded other indications that its inhabitants, the so-called Olmec people, also possessed knowledge of calendrics and hieroglyphic writing at an extremely early date. Largely on the basis of this fact, one school of scientific thought is of the opinion that the nucleus of Mayan culture may have actually originated in this area and spread from there toward the Petén. Such a possibility drew strong support from the late student of pre-Columbian art Miguel Covarrubias, but intensive study of this particular problem in recent years has failed to establish its validity beyond question.

On the basis of discoveries made at Uaxactún, archaeologists were now able to trace the advance of Mayan culture along specific fronts. Epigraphers were making important strides in fitting the numerous hieroglyphic monuments into an over-all chronological framework. Studies of architecture, sculpture, and ceramic sequences began to reveal the obscure routes along which the unique manifestations of Mayan civilization had spread outward. And much that was previously unknown concerning the traditions and motivating factors which had molded their way of life could be implied by careful analysis of the material remains laid bare by increasingly widespread excavations.

One fact along this line of inquiry stood out above all others: from its inception Mayan social structure assumed the form of a rigid theocracy dominated by extremely powerful priesthoods. Evidence to support this conclusion was overwhelming. Without exception all of their buildings were of a religious nature—temples and palace-like structures intended solely for the enactment of ceremonials or as keeping places of sacred images. The ornate sculpture adorning them portrayed various Mayan gods or was symbolic representations of supernatural connotation. And the entire body of hieroglyphic inscriptions thus far deciphered has borne solely upon matters of religious concern—astronomy, divination, ritualism, and deities.

It was demonstrated that throughout the environs occupied by the Maya at the height of their cultural florescence—over one hundred thousand square miles of varied and difficult terrain—the fundamental elements of sculpture, ceramics, and architecture showed a striking similarity. Especially was this found to be true regarding hieroglyphic writing and calendrics. Whether they appeared in the valley of the Motagua River in Honduras or far to the west in central Chiapas, the ideals expressed through these media remained largely unchanged for six hundred years. Remembering the veil of obscurity in which the fallen cities of the Maya were cloaked at the time of Stephens' explorations, such findings cannot fail to evoke renewed admiration for his prophetic appraisal: ". . . there is room for the belief that the whole of this country was once occupied by the same race, speaking the same language, or at least having the same written characters." Unknown to Stephens, he had touched upon the keystone of Mayan civilization—its initial vigor and ironically its eventual failing—the insuperable power of the guardian priests who directed its rise along inflexible lines of orthodoxy. Everything the Maya achieved had upon it the stamp of religious striving; it had evolved from a commonly shared and widespread source of inspiration. Leading the way before masses of humble, illiterate peasants, the priests established the tenets on which their existence was to rest throughout their history: the subjugation of life and property to religious mandates, the endless building of ceremonial centers, the adoration of the pantheon—especially the gods associated with crops, fertility, and rain—through rituals and offerings.

Mayan cities were indeed as Stephens had first perceived them to be: gigantic shrines to all that was darkly mysterious between known environment and the cosmic universe! They stood out starkly in fought-for clearings within the jungle— gleaming truncated pyramids, temples with stately, latticed roof combs, palaces and low-roofed buildings raised on platforms, lavishly adorned with sacred symbols and images of the patron deities to which they were consecrated. Many of the buildings exhibited brightly painted façades; others reflected only the natural colors of their materials. Principal edifices rose up from artificial acropolises to tower above the city's outline. Some buildings contained a single vaulted chamber; others consisted of a series of small, thick-walled rooms. Interiors were damp and poorly lighted as there were no windows or other means of ventilation—the only light and air penetrating the inner rooms filtered through the doorways.

Nor were temples alone the sole features of the cities. Almost always there were ball courts not unlike modern stadiums or amphitheaters, with long rows of stone benches and special observation points reserved for priests and royalty. Here spectators gathered to watch with passionate interest a ceremonial game in which a rubber ball (natural latex was known in Middle America at an early date) was passed through a stone ring in a manner similar to basketball. A score was seldom accomplished and the stakes were incredibly high—the winning player was sometimes awarded the clothing and jewelry of the spectators.

A number of cities contained remains of what appear to have been public baths, and structures intended for use as astronomical observatories are commonly found. Important buildings were provided with an efficient drainage system—stone troughs that carried off excess water to nearby streams or cement-lined reservoirs. And despite the absence of wheeled vehicles and draft animals, the Maya linked various sections of their cities with an elaborate network of roads and causeways constructed of finely cut stone over a gravel bedding. Frequently such roads connected distant cities as well, such as the intercity highway extending from Yaxuna in Yucatán to Cobá in Quintana Roo, a distance of sixty-two miles.

Only by years of toil could the Maya have hoped to create a ceremonial center in all its intended splendor. The jungle— the determination of which matched that of its inhabitants— had to be cleared and held back while the prodigious work of altering the land's natural contours and raising artificial mounds and acropolises progressed. Tons of stone were transported from quarries to the site on logrollers and fitted into place by grinding and chiseling. Laborers were conscripted from among the populace and worked with none but spiritual compensation. Yet the wave of ceaseless building went on!

Piedras Negras

Underlying the astounding growth through which the Maya passed lies one of the most perplexing factors encountered in Mayan research: How was it possible that so vast and energetic an empire was sustained by an agricultural system that never progressed beyond the most primitive stages of its inception? Irrigation and crop rotation were never practiced. Agricultural implements remained of the crudest possible variety. Clearing and withholding the jungle during the growing season required prodigious effort. Top soil was shallow and rock-filled, making the use of a plough virtually impossible, and five months of rain from May to October caused flooded conditions to alternate with long periods of dryness. Thus considered, the practice of extensive agriculture becomes an achievement of inordinate complexity. While in the Old World barren lands were transformed into fertile productivity by irrigation and diverting much of the work of cultivation to draft animals, the Maya could do little more than carry out their crude procedures and look upon the success or failure of each planting season as the province of their gods.

Strips of land known as milpas had to be felled and burned. Seeds were then planted using sticks with fire-hardened points. After several years, when the land's fertility was exhausted, the fields were abandoned and new milpas prepared elsewhere. By this method, which is still employed over much of Central America today, the Maya waged a continuous war against the jungle and sustained their way of life.

Aside from the restrictions placed on the Maya by the climatic rigors of their environment, other natural factors contributed measurably to their advancement. It seems reasonably certain that the centuries from A.D. 300 to 800—which witnessed the emergence of the Classic period—comprised an era of sustained peace unmarred by large-scale warfare, either among themselves or with groups beyond their immediate realm. A number of scholars attribute this uninterrupted development to the extreme geographical isolation of the Maya. The southern boundaries of their domain, they point out, were obstructed by the Guatemalan-Honduran highlands. Three quarters of the Yucatán Peninsula is surrounded by water; its land approaches from Mexico are sealed off by the tangled rain forests and swamps of Chiapas and Tabasco, thus permitting the Maya to evolve their unique culture relatively free of unwanted influences from outside sources. Undoubtedly there were political frictions which touched off limited conflicts and made necessary the maintenance of small armies, but the waging of war was never the stimulant to Mayan fortunes that it was to Egyptian and Greek.

As the Classic period marched forward, its denominators were the gradual spreading of established traditions, restless building, increasing population, and the exploration of new intellectual realms. Ideas were freely exchanged between cities, as were certain innovations in cosmology and ceremonialism. The priesthoods—whose power was by now unimpeachable—sought to apply their crafts to every facet of daily existence. They searched out the symbology and supernatural manifestations of the gods, their favors and displeasures, and the means by which they could be lured in living essence into the circle of human experience. By this endless pursuit of aesthetics Mayan civilization became a convincing testament to the power of religious absorption!

Priests stood at the helm of Mayan society. The cities were theirs alone; the populace continued to dwell, as they had from Archaic times, in thatched huts on the edge of outlying fields. Only the priests and segments of the ruling nobility entered the temples and shrines which were the labor of the awe-inspired multitudes.

For the ordinary man life remained a relentless cycle of tending his fields, manual labor, and participation in ceremonial rituals. There were never-ending tributes and sacrifices required by the priesthoods to support their sequestered realms of astronomy, mathematics, and philosophy. Yet, of such things, their subjects were permitted no knowledge whatsoever. Learning also was the sole dominion of the hierarchy.

In the beginning the masses were content to subject themselves completely to the will of the priests. Their desire, indeed their need, was to uphold the mandates of those whom they believed divinely chosen to guide their destinies; and for a while the priests held themselves apart from despotism and political tyranny. There was intoxication enough in the dawning of the Golden Age of which they had been the architects and guardians. Now it was upon them!

CHAPTER 7

The Classic Period:
Six Centuries of Achievement

ABOVE all else the Maya were to accomplish during the upward surge of Classic expansion, it was in the fields of calendrics and mathematics that their ingenuity was most pronounced. As these realms of knowledge were of the utmost importance—so far as their relation to supernatural factors was concerned—the priests expended unlimited effort toward their elucidation. Astronomy became the primary stimulus of their attainments, and the supreme proof of their intellectual abilities is evidenced by their mastery of its principles. Tirelessly they labored to explore the multiple aspects of time, to understand and placate its awesome influence upon the destiny of individuals and empire alike. And from their attempts evolved a calendrical lore which reached back millions of years in scope and encompassed a profoundly complex philosophy.

To the Maya, time was never a purely abstract denominator by which events were arranged into orderly sequences: rather it was an infinite beyond-world inhabited by omnipotent forces of creation and destruction. Its alternating cycles—the days, months, and years—were believed to bring with them the benevolence or evil of gods who bore them along their endlessly recurring cycles. Each bearer was the patron of a sacred number and assumed a form by which it could be portrayed in hieroglyphic inscriptions, and divisions of the calendar were regarded as "burdens" carried on the backs of these divine guardians of time. If a deity of malevolent intent happened to assume the burden of a particular cycle, grievous consequences could be expected until it was relinquished to a more provident bearer at the end of its natural course. Whether a certain month or year held promise of good or bad fortune was a matter predetermined by the temperament of the god on which it was borne.

It was a curious belief, and one which explains in part the far-reaching power of the priesthoods over the populace who must surely have deemed survival impossible without learned mediators to interpret the irascible tendencies of their gods. Only the astronomer-priests stood between normal continuation of life and catastrophes brought about by misjudging the inclinations of the divinities. Having recognized the varying aspects of the gods and plotted their restless paths along the highways of time and space, they alone could determine when it was that beneficial gods were in possession of specific periods; or, as was more often the case, when the greatest number of benevolent deities marched in conjunction with less sympathetic ones. Thus the Mayan obsession with time was very largely tantamount to a grand-scale quest for lucky and unlucky periods in the hope that once forewarned of future prospects their destiny could be guided along the most favorable possible course.

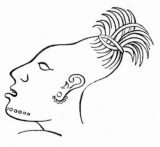

Piedras Negras

The Mayan calendar was the most accurate such invention known to the ancient world.* It was extremely complex in structure and interpretation, and consisted of a series of independently revolving "wheels" recording interrelated cycles of time. Two separate year measurements were observed: the *tzolkin* or sacred year made up of two hundred and sixty days, and a civil year known as a *haab* composed of eighteen months of twenty days each to which an extra month of five days was added, making a three-hundred-and-sixty-five-day year. The civil year was used in ordinary calendrical reckoning, whereas the shorter *tzolkin* determined matters pertaining to religious observances.

Each day and month was given a proper name and an identifying hieroglyph. There was a so-called "normal form" for each of these glyphs (usually an abstract design used in secular inscriptions) and a "head-variant form"—stylized images derived from humans, animals, and mythological creatures. Both forms functioned as graphic symbols in representing specific periods of time, and the "head-variant forms" were ordinarily reserved for inscriptions of a more formal or occult nature.

The basic unit of the Mayan calendar was the day or *kin*. Twenty *kins* comprised a *uinal* or month. Beginning with the *uinal,* the calendar was divided into cycles as follows:

18 *uinals*	= a *tun* (a year with the addition of five extra days)	
20 *tuns*	= a *katun* (7,200 days)	
20 *katuns*	= a *baktun* (144,000 days)	
20 *baktuns*	= a *pictun* (2,880,000 days)	
20 *pictuns*	= a *calabtun* (57,600,000 days)	
20 *calabtuns*	= a *kinchiltun* (1,152,000,000 days)	
20 *kinchiltuns*	= an *alautun* (23,040,000,000 days)	

* An extensive study of the Mayan calendar is found in *The Ancient Maya,* 1st edition, by Sylvanus G. Morley (Stanford, California: Stanford University Press, 1946); also in *The Rise and Fall of Maya Civilization,* by J. Eric Thompson (Norman: University of Oklahoma Press, 1954).

Each of these cycles revolved simultaneously, one within the other, expanding from *katuns* through *alautuns* by multiples of twenty. Each also had its identifying or accompanying glyph by which inscriptions relating to it can easily be recognized. Numerals accompanying these glyphs denoted the calendric cycles that had revolved since the earliest point at which the Maya began to record time. A typical date inscription as interpreted by archaeologists might read: 9.11.5.0.0 or nine elapsed *baktuns*, eleven *katuns*, five *tuns*, no *uinals*, and no *kins*—a date equivalent to A.D. 657. These "Long Count" or "Initial Series" inscriptions, as they are called, also contained glyphs denoting the day of the sacred year on which the date terminated; and were augmented by a "Supplementary Series" —glyphs pertaining to the age and position of the moon in relation to the accompanying Long Count. Eventually a simplified system of expressing dates known as the "Short Count" came into widespread use, which eliminated the representation of all but the day endings within a previously determined *katun*.

One of the major problems faced by epigraphers was that of arriving at the point in Mayan history from which time was first recorded. No correlation of the Mayan calendar with our own Gregorian system was possible without bringing the two systems to bear upon each other. The Gregorian calendar is oriented from the birth of Christ, but it was not known at what point this event coincided with Mayan chronology. The two calendrical systems were like halves of a gigantic slide rule; the problem was to bring their calibrations together to form corresponding equations.

In working out the calendric inscriptions it was discovered that every Initial Series sequence was counted from a cryptic date recorded as 13.0.0.0.0 4 *Ahua*, 8 *Cumhu*, which apparently marks the beginning of Mayan chronology. It is referred to as the "Zero Date" of all calendrical reckonings, and denotes a point roughly five thousand years in the past. Spinden interprets it literally as October 14, 3373 B.C. (it is 3113 B.C. according to the Goodman-Hernández-Thompson correlation). Oddly enough, this date was some three millennia *before* the earliest known dates on the Leyden Plate and Stela 9 from Uaxactún; thus archaeologists are agreed that it denotes a hypothetical event rather than one of historical actuality. Perhaps, as has been suggested by Morley, the Maya considered it the day of the world's creation or the birth date of their gods. It was from this point that the astronomer-priests began marking off divisions of lapsed and future time.

While unraveling the multiple complexities of the Mayan calendar, scholars were awakened as never before to the incredible technical prowess of the astronomer-priests that made possible its formulation. Over a period of many centuries they had meticulously observed and recorded the passage of celestial bodies back and forth across the skies—the "gods marching in never-ending relays." Using towers and raised platforms with pre-fixed lines of sight, their courses had been carefully plotted. Eventually accurate tables were devised for predicting solar and lunar eclipses, and specialized studies were concentrated on the synodical revolution of the planet Venus until the worship of the so-called Venus year became the inspiration of a highly covert cult.

Mayan astronomers had been well aware that seemingly minute errors in dividing time into its recurring cycles would eventually multiply irreconcilable flaws. As a result of cautious observation the margin of error in their computations was incredibly slight, and corrections were made to allow for the discrepancies brought about by leap years and other synodical variations. And always there remained the difficult problem of synchronizing the various calendrical divisions with one another, as well as to enmesh the three-hundred-and-sixty-five-day civil year with the two-hundred-and-sixty-day sacred year.

Without a workable mathematical system the Maya would have been hopelessly at sea in such endeavors.

Like the astronomical glyphs, two methods were employed in recording numerical notations: elaborate head-variant numerals and a more commonly used system of bars and dots. A dot was equivalent to one unit, and a bar was equal to five. Numbers from one to nineteen were written in varying combinations of each:

1	6	11	16
2	7	12	17
3	8	13	18
4	9	14	19
5	10	15	0

Numbers above nineteen were noted according to their placement in vertical columns, and each ascending position increased in value by multiples of twenty from bottom to top. Numbers placed opposite a specific position were multiplied by its corresponding multiple of twenty; the column was then added to formulate the sum total.

One of the most notable innovations brought about by the Maya in the field of mathematics was the principle of the zero. This abstract concept, essential to all but the most simplified calculations, had eluded discovery by the most advanced civilizations of the Old World. At only one other place in antiquity—among the ancient Hindus—was its use independently evolved. Subsequently it passed to Arabia and was acquired by the Moors who introduced it into Europe during the Middle Ages, but the Maya were making use of the zero at a date far earlier than even Hindu mathematicians. It was represented in their inscriptions by means of a shell, an open hand, or one of several variant glyphs.

As we have seen, the motivating factor underlying the rise of Mayan civilization was one of religious expression, and archaeologists have demonstrated that the complexity of religious manifestations advanced hand in hand with the development of calendrics, mathematics, and hieroglyphic writing. Architecture and stone sculpture added to these a third dimension—the means of solidifying and preserving sacred images and inscriptions.

Unquestionably this religious fervor had seized the Maya at a very early date in their history. Sylvanus Morley writes that by the fourth century A.D.—at the very dawn of the Classic period—Mayan religion had already "... become a highly developed cult based upon a fusion of the primitive personification of nature with a more sophisticated philosophy, built around a deification of the heavenly bodies and a worship of time. This religion, while shared with the common people, was highly esoteric in nature. It was interpreted and served by a closely organized priesthood composed of astronomers, mathematicians, prophets, and ritualists, and, as it grew more complex, by skilled administrators and statesmen." *

From post-Conquest documents and a careful interpretation of hieroglyphic texts, students have gleaned a considerable amount of knowledge pertaining to the nature of deities, mythology, and religious practices. Mayan cosmology records the creation of the world by a god known as Hunab Ku. So important were Hunab Ku's functions, and so sacred was his realm, that he is believed to have played little part in the everyday affairs of the populace.

* Reprinted from *The Ancient Maya,* by Sylvanus G. Morley, with the permission of the publishers, Stanford University Press. Copyright 1946, 1947, and 1956 by the Board of Trustees of Leland Stanford Junior University. *The Ancient Maya* contains a more detailed study of Mayan religion than can be included here.

Residing beneath Hunab Ku in the Mayan pantheon was an array of gods whose functions and character were extremely varied. All of them apparently possessed human attributes, both good and evil, and they assumed anthropomorphic forms by which they can easily be recognized when encountered in hieroglyphic inscriptions. Again, however, archaeologists have had to rely upon the writings of Bishop Landa and the few surviving native manuscripts for most of their information concerning this important cultural facet. Landa took particular pains to examine the nature of Mayan deities because of his desire to eradicate their influence among his subjects.

Of first rank was the god Itzamna, who, it is believed, was the son of the mighty Hunab Ku. He appears as an aged man with toothless jaws, hollow cheeks, and a protruding nose. Itzamna was regarded as second only to his father in the powers of creation. He was the "inventor of books and writing," and was addressed variously as Lord of the Day, Lord of the Night and the Heavens. He frequently consorted with the moon goddess known as Ixchel.

Another powerful deity was Chac, who presided over the four cardinal directions, and to whom the peasants appealed for rain when planting their fields, for Chac's concern was with the earth's fecundity. Beside him the youthful God of Maize vied for the adoration of the agrarian peasants. His slender profile, beneath a headdress of maize ears or wearing a florid serpentine crown, was always associated with agriculture to which he imparted his blessings. Also prominent was the much dreaded Ah Puch, the Lord of Death, whose skeleton-like form symbolized for the Maya the fearful mysteries of death; and his abettor—the "Black Captain"—whose wrath brought about war and malevolent deeds.

Other gods—those of Wind, Human Sacrifice, and Celestial Bodies, and the goddesses of Fertility and Suicide—exerted a powerful influence over the Maya. As they envisioned the universe as made up of thirteen "upper worlds" and nine "under-worlds," a patron god was attributed to each of these levels of existence as well. Added to these were the various number gods, deities associated with the calendar (those of the days, months, and years), and countless spirits of lesser significance.

Inherent in the nature and behavior of Mayan gods was an active dualism which Morley has described as "the eternal struggle between the powers of good and evil over the destiny of man. The benevolent gods, bringing thunder, lightning, and rain, fructify the corn and ensure plenty. The malevolent ones, whose attributes are death and destruction, cause drought, hurricanes, and war. . . . This contest is depicted in the codices, where Chac, the rain god, is shown caring for a young tree, while behind him follows Ah Puch, the death god, who breaks the tree in two. This balance of good against evil in the struggle for the soul of man is a contrast found in many religions, some far older than Christianity." *

The Maya also shared with many other peoples the belief that the soul was perpetuated after death in a state of serene pleasure or eternal torment, according to the nature of one's deeds and the measure of his devotion to religious ideals. Lavish delights awaited those who so earned them; the damned were committed to Mitnal, the Mayan hell—a demon-infested wasteland of never-ending cold and hunger. Suicide, especially by hanging, was looked upon as the greatest possible measure of personal sacrifice. It insured the unqualified pleasures of immortality.

Aside from what can be inferred from material remains—knowledge pertaining largely to astronomy, mathematics, and astrology—much concerning other facets of Mayan thought and philosophy remains in obscurity. Hieroglyphic inscriptions

* Reprinted from *The Ancient Maya,* by Sylvanus G. Morley, with the permission of the publishers, Stanford University Press. Copyright 1946, 1947, and 1956 by the Board of Trustees of Leland Stanford Junior University.

have revealed certain broad concepts in this regard, and some insight has been gained by observing the behavior and traditions of the contemporary descendants of the ancient Maya. But at best these findings are desultory and influenced by centuries of Christian teaching. Greek and Roman thought—the entire outpouring of the most gifted intellects of their respective ages—has come down to us intact to exert a profound influence upon the course of Western Civilization. So, too, have large segments of Oriental philosophy. Yet from the Maya, who matched and in some respects excelled these peoples in the brilliance of their intellectual achievements, historians can draw upon little more than tantalizing samples pertaining to much of their non-material culture.

Scholars can readily interpret what is preserved in stone. But what of those more perishable arts which are often a greater measure of achievement? What had the Maya sought to express through music and dance? What ideals were embodied in literature and folklore in the remote centuries before alien influences began to invalidate their intrinsic imagery and values? If such surviving examples of their literary abilities as the *Popol Vuh* and *The Annals of the Cakchiquels* are accurate indications of their facility with language, then their potential legacy in this realm alone was immeasurable. On the sole merit of material remains the Maya were long ago likened to the Athenians: were it possible to reconstruct the full range of their intellectual endeavors such parallels would in all probability extend infinitely beyond these manifestations. Unfortunately, the priesthoods utilized their knowledge of hieroglyphic writing almost exclusively to record matters pertaining to astronomy. Little else can be read from the existing inscriptions, and the surviving peasant population can offer virtually no insight into the very distant past. Vast segments of Mayan civilization were buried with the last of its guardian priests, perhaps never to be reclaimed.

It is certain that the populace in general had little comprehension of the broader philosophic aspects of their faith or the intellectual pursuits of the priesthoods. Mass participation was limited to communal rites of placation focused primarily upon those deities believed to influence the soil, crops, and rain. A ceremonial calendar of events was rigorously observed: the arrival of numerous sacred days necessitated the enactment of rituals, as did the ending of *katun* cycles, the new year, the beginning of each month, the dedication of monuments and buildings, the seasons of planting and harvest, and countless other occasions acknowledged by feasts, the presentation of offerings, prayers, and dances. On such days the ceremonial enclosures were crowded with participants, whose homage was directed by the priests through widely varied ritualism which included such practices as fasting and rites of purification, the burning of copal incense, bloodletting, dances, chanting, and final consummate feasts.

But as the scope of priestly strivings broadened, as city after city came into being with expanding populations and deepening economic tensions, the Maya began to question the sufficiency of mundane offerings and long-formulated rituals in maintaining the support of the divinities. Was not life itself a more fitting tribute? Neighboring tribes on the Mexican plateau had long before turned to human sacrifice in their quest for divine favor—the wholesale dedication of warriors taken in battle expressly toward such ends. Whether of their own volition or by the inference of these Mexican tribes, human life itself became the ultimate offer of appeasement among the Maya.

Morley gives a vivid description of the method by which such sacrifices were usually carried out: *

* Reprinted from *The Ancient Maya*, by Sylvanus G. Morley, with the permission of the publishers, Stanford University Press. Copyright 1946, 1947, and 1956 by the Board of Trustees of Leland Stanford Junior University.

The intended victim, after being stripped, painted blue [the sacrificial color], and having a special peaked head-dress set on his head, was led to the place of sacrifice. This was usually either the temple courtyard or the summit of the pyramid supporting the temple. The evil spirits were first expelled and the altar, usually a convex stone that curved the victim's breast upward, was smeared with the sacred blue paint. The four *chacs,* also painted blue, next grasped the victim by his arms and legs and stretched him on his back over the altar. The *nacom* advanced with the sacrificial flint knife and plunged it into the victim's ribs just below the left breast. Thrusting his hand into the opening, he pulled out the still-beating heart and handed it to the *chilan,* or officiating priest, who smeared blood on the idol to whom the sacrifice was being made. If the victim had been sacrificed on the summit of a pyramid, the *chacs* threw the corpse to the court below, where priests of a lower rank skinned the body, except for the hands and feet. The *chilan,* having removed his sacrificial vestments, arrayed himself in the skin of the victim and solemnly danced with the spectators. If the sacrificial victim had been a valiant and brave soldier, his body was sometimes divided and eaten by the nobles and other spectators. The hands and feet were reserved for the *chilan,* and, if the victim was a prisoner of war, his captor wore certain of his bones as a mark of prowess. Women and children were as frequently sacrificed as men.

Bishop Landa provided a lurid description of yet another form of human sacrifice in the pages of his *Relación de las cosas de Yucatán:*

If he was to be sacrificed by arrows, they stripped him naked and anointed his body with a blue color, and put a pointed cap on his head. When they had reached the victim, all of them, armed with bows and arrows, made a solemn dance with him around the stake, and while dancing they put him up on it, all of them continuing to dance and look-ing at him. The foul priest in vestments went up and wounded the victim with an arrow in the parts of shame, whether it were a man or woman, and drew blood and came down and anointed the face of the idol with it. And making a sign to the dancers, as they passed rapidly before him still dancing, they began one after another to shoot at his heart, which had been marked beforehand with a white sign. And in this manner they made his whole chest one point like a hedgehog full of arrows.

Mayan society was never closely integrated. Between the ruling hierarchy and the common people there existed inflexible barriers of caste and training. Each group lived at extreme poles from the other. The peasantry could look forward to little more than a life of servitude bound up in the duties of farming and the demands of the priesthoods, while the ruling classes enjoyed the copious fruits of their adoration.

Both the priests and the nobility established lines of heredity through which their offices were passed on to succeeding generations. Bishop Landa, writing of the native priesthoods in Yucatán, stated: "They taught the sons of the other priests and the second sons of the lords who brought them from their infancy, if they saw that they had an inclination for this profession; ... and his [the high priest's] sons or his nearest relatives succeeded him in office."

The functions of the high priest were multifold in nature. Landa wrote:

> He was much respected by the lords ... besides the offerings, the lords made him presents and all the priests of the town brought contributions to him. ... In him was the key of their learning and it was to these matters that they mostly dedicated themselves; and they gave advice to the lords and replies to their questions. ... They provided priests for the towns when they were needed, examining them in the sciences and ceremonies and committed to them the duties of their office, and set good examples to people and provided them with books and sent them forth. And they employed themselves in the duties of the temples

and in teaching their sciences as well as writing books about them. . . .

The sciences which they taught were the computation of the years, months, and days, the festivals and ceremonies, the administration of the sacraments, the fateful days and seasons, their methods of divination and their prophecies, events and the cures for diseases and their antiquities, and how to read and write with their letters and characters with which they wrote, and drawings which illustrate the meaning of their writings.

Aiding the high priests with their functions were *chilanes* or prophets, whose duty was to commune directly with the gods and interpret portents and mystical omens. Other classes of priests—the *nacom* and *chacs*—assisted in matters of ritual and sacrifice.

Archaeology confirms the assumption that the priesthoods reigned supreme in the scale of Mayan society; priests are always represented on sculptured monuments as robed in lavish costumes, laden with jewelry, surrounded by offerings, seated on thronelike platforms, or otherwise occupying places of utmost prestige. Morley confirms that their "knowledge of astronomy, their ability to predict eclipses, their penetration into every phase of life, made them feared and respected and gave them a hold on the superstitions of the people equaled by that of no other class." *

Next in order of importance were the nobility in whose hands the problems of temporal government rested. Each city —the principal religious center and its outlying peasant districts—was governed by a supreme lord or chieftain known as the *halach uinic* (which means the true man). Assisting him in the affairs of state was a group of less powerful chiefs, the *batabs,* whose duties corresponded to those of local adminis-

---

* Reprinted from *The Ancient Maya,* by Sylvanus G. Morley, with the permission of the publishers, Stanford University Press. Copyright 1946, 1947, and 1956 by the Board of Trustees of Leland Stanford Junior University.

trators. Broadly speaking, they were the village "mayors." Their authority extended to matters of executive and judicial importance, and they were permitted to command small contingents of soldiers. Below the *batabs* were a number of town councilors and minor deputies whose primary duty was to carry out the orders of the governing lords.

As yet there is no conclusive evidence that the far-flung network of city-states was ever welded into a single confederation by unified political control. Each important city apparently remained autonomous from its neighboring centers, independently governed by its own nobility and priests. Scholarly viewpoints on this question have differed along two routes of speculation: One suggests that the marked similarity in such manifestations as architecture, art, calendrics, and hieroglyphics —and the era of apparent political tranquillity which allowed their development—were due in part to the powerful direction of a centralized government dominated by a succession of rulers who were either secular or theocratic in nature. Opponents of this view have argued that the homogeneous character of Mayan culture resulted from commonly shared religious ideals rather than political unification—there is impressive evidence to support the latter view. On these points, however, much is still to be learned.

Scarcely anything can be glimpsed from archaeological evidence concerning the individual lives of the common people. Inscriptions and pictorial art do not portray their roles or condition. Remains of their dwellings—fragile structures of stucco and thatch—have not survived alongside the ceremonial centers whose number and impressiveness stand as material testimony of their devotion to the regnant beliefs that influenced every facet of their lives.

Areas of former peasant occupation, which were almost always in close proximity to the outlying milpas, are recognizable to the trained eyes of archaeologists by refuse mounds and the faint outlines of their characteristic habitations. Houses of exactly the same type are used by their present-day descendants—rectangular enclosures made either of stucco or packed earth reinforced by a framework of laced poles. Occasionally the walls were constructed of stone, and the roofing consisted of tightly woven thatch.

Excavations of these dwelling sites have underlined the simple existence of the lay populace: large amounts of broken pottery—most of it utilitarian ware used for cooking or storage—are found along with grinding stones, a variety of implements such as axes, flint knives, scrapers, awls, and clay figurines representing deities. But conspicuously absent from these prosaic remnants are objects indicative of varying degrees of material wealth among the peasant population; everything points to absolute community of ownership. Nor can it be doubted that the relatively small nucleus of priest-intellectuals —on whose efforts the glory of Mayan civilization rested—deliberately perpetuated the humble state of their subjects. Upon their economic productivity and willingness to carry out required tasks depended the leisure of the priesthoods to explore science and aesthetics.

Enslaved as they were to religious mandates and to the hierarchy who formulated them, the energies of the populace were directed toward the ceaseless round of tributes and physical labor required to support and expand the religious centers. Landa tells us that the houses of the ruling lords were constructed by the peasants "at their own expense," that they planted, tilled, and harvested their fields [those belonging to the lords], and shared with them the bounty from hunting and fishing. It is a fair estimate that two thirds of every regular harvest went to support the hierarchy, and there were required tributes of items such as salt, copal incense, ornaments, cloth, wild game, fruit, and honey. Lands were communally

owned; no individual was permitted to own property in his
own name.

Piedras Negras

Yet no society, however stringent its ruling hierarchy may
be, exists without expressions of folk culture. Fortunately
Bishop Landa recorded a wealth of such information relating
to the Maya in his history of Yucatán, and it is largely from
his manuscript that our knowledge of the peasant class is
derived. While it is true that Landa's observations date from
the period immediately after the Conquest, it is doubtful
whether the pattern of daily life had altered very much from
that of more ancient times. Now and then references in Landa's
text have been borne out by actual excavations, and many of the
practices noted by him survive among the present-day inhabitants of Yucatán. For instance, their traditional dress, techniques of weaving and pottery making, methods of agriculture,
and the pattern of life in general are virtually unchanged.
Other historians of the sixteenth and seventeenth centuries
have amplified Landa's account, and by checking their observations against these earlier sources, archaeologists have been
able to reconstruct in part the manners and traditions by
which the Mayan populace ordered their lives.

The birth of a child was perhaps the Maya's greatest source
of personal happiness; it signified a direct sanction of the
divinities, especially of the goddess Ixchel. Infants were given
a childhood name by a priest who also devised a horoscope to
aid in their upbringing. Later they added the family names of

both parents and assumed a nickname by which they were known to intimate persons. One's birthday was counted from the day of the *tzolkin,* the ceremonial year, on which he was born. From this could also be foretold which of the patron deities were likely to favor or malign the youth throughout his lifetime.

By nature the Maya were unusually gentle and temperate. Landa's observations frequently reveal their generosity and willingness to subject personal desires to the over-all well-being of the community; in revealing the enormity of public works archaeology resoundly confirmed their unquestioned devotion to commonly shared ideals. Children were brought up to be obedient not only to their elders, but to the more important restrictions placed on them by the ruling hierarchy.

It was greatly desired to be cross-eyed, so a nodule of resin or a small bead was attached to the child's hair and allowed to fall between the eyes. The heads of infants were tightly lashed to a board in order to flatten and elongate the forehead; this, too, was considered a measure of special beauty. Both men and women filed their teeth to sharp points, and covered their faces and bodies with decorative scars and tattoos. Persons of high rank often inlaid their teeth with turquoise, jade, or shell.

Men dressed in simple breechclouts woven of cotton and rawhide sandals; the women robed themselves in loose-fitting mantles and shawls. The typical clothing of the peasants could scarcely be compared to the ornate vestments of the privileged minority who went about swathed in richly embroidered cloth, elaborate capes made of feathers or jaguar skins, and arrayed in ornaments of carved jade, turquoise, gold, and inlaid shell.

Morley tells us that when a boy reached the age of five, a small white bead was braided in his hair. Girls were given a string from which dangled a red shell to wear about the waist. These were symbols of virginity, and could not be removed without dishonor until the rite which marked the beginning of adolescence. Drawing upon the observations of Bishop Landa, Morley recounts the interesting details of this ritual in his book, *The Ancient Maya:* *

The day of the puberty ceremony was carefully selected; pains were taken to ascertain that it would not be an unlucky day. A principal man of the town was chosen as sponsor for the children participating; his duty was to assist the priest during the ceremony and to furnish the feast. Four honorable old men were selected as *chacs,* to assist the priest. . . . On the appointed day, all assembled in the court of the sponsor's house, which had been newly swept and strewn with fresh leaves. An old man was assigned to act as godfather for the boys, and an old woman as godmother for the girls. When this was done the priest purified the dwelling and conducted a ceremony to expel the evil spirit.

When the spirit had been expelled, the court was swept out again, fresh leaves were strewn about, and mats were spread on the floor. The priest changed his vestments to a handsome jacket and a miter-like headdress of colored feathers, taking in his hand an aspergillum for sprinkling holy water. This latter consisted of a finely worked short stick with rattlesnake tails hanging from it. The *chacs* approached the children and placed on their heads pieces of white cloth, which their mothers had brought for this purpose. The older children were asked if they had committed any sin or obscene act. If they had, they were separated from the others. . . . This concluded, the priest ordered everyone to be seated and to preserve absolute silence, and after pronouncing a benediction on the children, he sat down. The sponsor of the ceremony, with a bone given him by the priest, tapped each child nine times on the forehead, moistening the forehead, the face, and the spaces between the fingers and toes with water.

---

* Reprinted from *The Ancient Maya,* by Sylvanus G. Morley, with the permission of the publishers, Stanford University Press. Copyright 1946, 1947, and 1956 by the Board of Trustees of Leland Stanford Junior University.

After this anointing, the priest removed the white cloths from the children's heads. The children then gave the *chacs* some feathers and cacao beans which they had brought as gifts. The priest next cut the white beads from the boys' heads. The attendants carried pipes which they smoked from time to time, giving each child a puff of smoke. Gifts of food, brought by the mothers, were distributed to the children, and a wine offering was made to the gods; this wine had to be drunk at one draught by a specially appointed official.

The young girls were then dismissed, each mother removing from her daughter the red shell which had been worn as a symbol of purity. With this, the girl was considered to have reached a marriageable age. The boys were dismissed next. When the children had withdrawn from the court, their parents distributed among the spectators and officials pieces of cotton cloth which they had brought as gifts. The ceremony closed with feasting and heavy drinking. . . .

Marriage was permitted any time after the puberty ceremony, although generally it did not occur until an average age of twenty. Arrangements were usually made through the parents with the fathers selecting the future wives of their sons. It was important to choose a girl of equal background who was properly trained in the domestic duties and modest behavior befitting an ideal wife. One had to be careful not to violate certain restrictions which prohibited unions between persons related by clan membership or prior marriage. Such matters took time and followed a devious procedure of bargaining; often a skilled matchmaker was engaged to represent the bridegroom in the important question of a worth-while dowry. After the wedding the groom was required to dwell with his wife's parents for several years to assist his father-in-law, and thus prove his abilities. He was then free to establish a separate home with his wife. Marriage could be dissolved at any time by a simple declaration on the part of either the husband or the wife.

Landa's description of a typical Mayan settlement indicates that social prestige was determined by the location of one's dwelling: "In the middle of the town were the temples with beautiful plazas, and all around the temples stood the houses of the lords and the priests, and then of the most important people. Thus came the houses of the richest and of those who were held in the highest estimation nearest to these, and at the outskirts of the town were the houses of the lower classes. And the wells, if there were but few of them, were near the houses of the lords...."

While the women attended to the duties of their homes— cooking, weaving cloth, and caring for their children—the men's province was that of the fields. Before the sun rose each morning they left their houses for the milpas. It was well to work several hours before the tropical sun reached its noon zenith when its rays were beneficial only to the sun-loving maize. Often they rested in the shade of the nearby forest. Sometimes they dissolved a lump of corn-meal dough which they called *pozole* in a gourd filled with water and drank it to refresh themselves. Cutting and burning the milpas and holding back the jungle from the growing plants were difficult tasks; they had no tools to work with except stone axes and pointed sticks. Besides the sacred corn they raised red and black beans, squash, melons, tomatoes, and sweet potatoes. Each day, before their labor began, the men prayed to the earth gods and burned copal before images which stood nearby watching over the neat rows of growing plants.

Rarely was there time for idle pursuits. When the growing season ended, the energies of the populace were requisitioned by the hierarchy and directed toward programs of supervised labor. The task of quarrying stone, of erecting new temples, and laying roads and causeways through the forests was endless during the six hundred years in which the Mayan empire achieved its greatest degree of expansion. Ever-widening horizons in every field of endeavor made necessary relentless projects of building in order to solidify the underlying principles of their advancement. Each new calendric cycle was commemorated in stone, every god was portrayed repetitiously in sculptured images, and each new cult was provided a shrine in which its attendant priests could enact rites and pursue their study. Underlying all of this was the devotion of a populace who were denied even a cursory insight into the specialized knowledge of their spiritual mentors.

When sickness occurred, a medicine man or sorcerer was called upon to examine the victim. He might prescribe a dosage of secretly blended herbs—often with beneficial results—or invoke magic intended to drive away evil spirits which were believed to be the cause of disease. When the illness was beyond hope of cure, he would prophesy how long the patient yet had to live and what his prospects were regarding the afterlife.

The dead were cremated or buried beneath the floors of their houses, which were usually abandoned by the surviving members of a family. The body was wrapped in cloth and the mouth filled with ground corn and a polished stone. Into the grave were placed clay idols, offerings of corn, and objects which the deceased had frequently used during his lifetime. Even to this day the Maya look upon death with abject terror. Landa stated: "It was indeed a thing to see the sorrow and the cries which they made for their dead, and the great grief it caused them. During the day they wept for them in silence; and at night with loud and very sad cries, so that it was pitiful to hear them. And they passed many days in deep sorrow. They made abstinences and fasts for the dead, especially the husband or wife; and they said that the devil had taken him away since they thought that all evils came to them from him, and especially death."

Overwhelming mysteries surrounded and awed the Mayan peasant: the movements of the heavens, the sunrise, thunder and wind, birth and death itself, these were the manifest powers of the gods thrown up like an infinite mirror in which was reflected the frailty of his existence. Entrapped in fear, the farmer raised his eyes beyond his fields and through the forest to the gleaming spires of sacred temples where he sought the assurance of those whose knowledge permitted them greater insight into unknown realms. To achieve that assurance no privation was too costly.

Willingly he joined in the building of the holy cities. Many of his days were given to participation in ceremonials and prayer. At night there was comfort in remembering the tributes he had placed before the temples. His life was spent in flight from an age-old fear of the unknown. It had followed man from the dawn of his existence; to escape it had been the universal inspiration of his religions. For the Maya it was the foundation upon which was wrought an eloquent civilization.

CHAPTER 8

Palenque Yields a "Royal" Tomb

•

AT the far western boundary of the ancient Mayan domain, in what is now the Mexican state of Chiapas, lie the ruins of Palenque. Along with the nearby cities of Yaxchilán and Piedras Negras in the valley of the Usumacinta River, Palenque's creation climaxed the Classic expansion in the western half of the Mayan empire. Its sedate buildings reflect the ultimate ideals of architectural and sculptural expression toward which its builders had steadily progressed.

Palenque had been a religious center of imposing magnitude. Its exact boundaries are still obscured by the encircling rain forest, but the shapeless mounds of rubble that were once its resplendent structures extend three and a half miles west and two miles east of the principal ceremonial complex.

In 1923 the Mexican government assigned the American archaeologist Franz Blom to begin excavating certain of the city's important structures. Blom's primary undertaking was to lay bare and reconstruct portions of the Great Palace as near its original splendor as possible. In recent years the archaeological zone of Palenque was designated as a national monument, and steps were taken to eliminate the arduous journey formerly required to visit the site.

Now it can be reached via the Southeast Railroad, either from Campeche on the western coast of the Yucatán Peninsula, or Allende in Veracruz. A landing field has also been opened in the nearby village of Santo Domingo del Palenque, from which the site acquired its name. A narrow road leading to the ruins winds out from the sparse settlement along what was once an Indian footpath. A three-mile drive through luxuriant forests and broad milpas brings the ancient city into view with startling suddenness.

Directly ahead rises the Great Palace supported by a steeply inclined acropolis which has crumbled away in places, exposing a series of subterranean passages. At its southwest corner the Temple of the Inscriptions crowns a high-vaulted terraced pyramid, with broad steps leading to its summit. A narrow stream known as the Otolum divides the city almost in half; an aqueduct formerly diverted its water nearer the Palace, and its shallow bed was roofed over with cemented stones to form an unbroken causeway linking its opposite sides. East of the Otolum a number of smaller, superbly designed temples lie on grass-covered mounds at the base of the Tumbála Hills which enclose the city's southern and western approaches. Still more structures are visible before the broad savannah that descends northward toward the Bay of Campeche, eighty miles distant. Surrounding the exposed limits of the city are dozens of rubble-covered mounds, reaffirming here as elsewhere throughout the Mayan area the enormity of the problems still confronting archaeologists.

What is presently known of Palenque's role in Mayan history has resulted from the efforts of numerous investigators pursuing varied phases of research. Blom opened the way for the application of modern archaeological techniques during his excavation of the Great Palace. Previously the American archaeologist William H. Holmes had carried out an exhaustive preliminary survey of the entire city. Teobert Maler devoted a considerable amount of time to an examination of the site during his explorations in the Usumacinta Valley. Noted Mayan scholars such as Alfred Tozzer, Herbert Spinden, and Sylvanus Morley have subjected Palenque to intensive research

during the past twenty-five years. And the studies made by
J. Eric Thompson of Palenque's superb hieroglyphic inscriptions were of immeasurable value in reconstructing the city's
archaeological lineage.

In 1934 the Mexican National Institute of Anthropology
and History appointed the archaeologist Miguel Fernández to
direct a series of excavations aimed at permanently restoring
Palenque's most important structures. Shortly after Fernández'
untimely death in 1945 the continuation of the project fell into
the capable hands of Alberto Ruz Lhuillier. Ruz was possessed
of tireless enthusiasm and intense determination. It was fateful
indeed that he should have plied his talents to Palenque; his
faculties were perfectly suited to the task that befell him. He
was on the threshold of a startling discovery.*

The object of Ruz' efforts was the further restoration of the
city's most important monuments—eight pyramid temples and
sections of the Palace complex. As field work was restricted to
periods of four months—because of hampering rains that
deluge the area throughout most of the year—it was to be an
undertaking of indefinite duration. With a force of Indians
recruited from the nearby village, Ruz set to work erecting a
permanent building to serve as a camp and laboratory. After
that began the drudging labor of felling the jungle that engulfed the ruins before actual excavations could proceed.

Ruz was particularly intrigued by the Temple of the Inscriptions—the magnificent structure standing atop a seventy-foot
pyramid in which Stephens had discovered the delicately etched
hieroglyphic tablets. It was the floor of the interior chamber
that first alerted Ruz' curiosity. The fact that it was made of
carefully fitted flagstones immediately set it apart; ordinarily
the Maya utilized stucco for the floors of their buildings. Near

---

* Señor Ruz has written about his findings at Palenque in "The Mystery of
the Temple of the Inscriptions" (*Archaeology*, Vol. 6 [1953]) and "The Mystery
of the Mayan Temple" (*The Saturday Evening Post*, August 29, 1953).

the center of the room was an inordinately large stone with three pairs of holes drilled at its opposite ends. These, in turn, had been fitted with stone plugs to conceal their presence from view. Archaeologists had long debated their possible significance, but to no definite conclusion. Ruz was not content to rest the matter on speculation alone. It was possible, he concluded, that the curious plugged holes had held a religious connotation for the Maya, such as symbolic entrances to the Underworld. Perhaps they had borne in some way upon astronomical observations. Or were they a key to some undisclosed architectural feature within the building itself?

Ultimately his re-examination of the chamber revealed a circumstance overlooked in earlier explorations: there were positive indications that the walls of the room continued on beneath the level of the floor, as though a second room lay below the upper chamber. Ruz decided to raise the drilled stone from the floor on a vague hunch that such had been the original purpose of the holes. Chisels broke the lime mortar from the interstices between the flagstones and the floor of the temple was opened.

Below it was what appeared to be the outline of a narrow passageway completely filled with rubble. At first it was impossible to determine whether it actually led to a lower room or was merely a small subsurface crypt. But as the debris was cleared from the opening there appeared the outline of steps made of stones covered with stucco. It was obvious that this was in a fact a stairway which led down through a vaulted tunnel into the core of the pyramid. Ruz was determined to follow the passage to its end, even though there was no assurance that the exhausting labor required to accomplish this would be justified by his findings. But the existence of an elaborate subterranean stairway—a feature never before encountered in a Mayan structure—presented irresistible possibilities.

The work of clearing the passage proceeded with maddening slowness. The heavy stones blocking the stairway had to be loosened and hauled up with ropes and pulleys. Heat and depressing humidity within the passage were stifling. Fumes given off by the excavators' gasoline lamp and clouds of choking dust made it impossible to remain in the tunnel for long periods at a time. At the conclusion of the first season's work, twenty-three steps had been laid bare and the outline of the descending vault was essentially clear.

Even now there was no way of knowing toward what the passageway was leading, but something had come to light that rekindled Ruz' expectations. Along one wall of the passage was a curious kind of duct—a square shaft made of small cut stones held together with lime mortar. What purpose it might have served was not known, but there obviously had to be some motive for its construction concealed still lower in the pyramid's depths.

As the passage was deepened the obstructing stones were heavier and tightly cemented by lime salts deposited during the centuries they had lain undisturbed. There could be no question that the tortuous difficulty in reaching the bottom of the stairway resulted from a deliberate intent on the part of its builders. When the passageway had served its purpose— whatever that might have been—it had been sealed against further intrusion by piling masses of stones and rubble along its entire length. Then the flagstone had been set in place over the entrance in the temple floor, and the drilled holes used to lower it into position were filled with stone plugs. Once Palenque was abandoned, the knowledge of the subterranean vault vanished with its inhabitants. That much of the enigma now seemed certain.

At the conclusion of the third season's work the stairway was opened to a depth of almost seventy feet. Still there was not the slightest clue to its original purpose. No inscriptions had been found along the walls; not a single fragment of sculpture had come to light in the tons of debris lifted from the mouth of the tunnel. Only the perfectly formed steps dropping lower into the core of the pyramid and the curious square duct which continued on into the seemingly endless wall of rubble. Ruz had been minutely thorough in his search thus far. He had overlooked nothing. There was simply no choice but to continue digging.

During the following season—in the fall of 1952—the excavators broke through into a corridor blocked at one end by a thick wall of tightly packed rubble. Beyond that they encountered still another wall of cemented stones. Immediately in front of the second wall lay a square stone box; its contents offered the first reward for the exhausting labor expended in clearing the passageway. Inside was a cache of jade ornaments —highly polished beads, pendants, earplugs, and buttons. Beneath these were two exquisitely painted ceramic plates and a single gleaming pearl half an inch in diameter. Unquestionably the objects had been intended as ceremonial offerings, but toward what amorphic end had they been left behind in the otherwise empty corridor? Before the men huddled together in the dimly lighted vault was still that massive second wall through which they would have to pass if the widening dilemma was ever to make archaeological sense.

According to Ruz' own account, "the wall turned out to be more than twelve feet thick; breaking through it took a full week of the hardest labor of the entire expedition. The mortar held so firmly that the stones often broke before they separated; and the wet lime burned and cracked the workmen's hands. Finally we got through and came upon a rude masonry box, or chest."

Inside the chest were the remains of six human skeletons that had been covered over with a layer of mortared stones. No ornaments or offerings were found in the multiple coffin, and the bodies were those of youths whose death had occurred in the years of early adulthood. The whole scene before Ruz and his companions had the overtones of a deliberate act. "Unquestionably," he wrote, "this was a human sacrifice, young persons whose spirits were forever to guard and attend him for whom all this entire massive pyramid had been made— and whom we now soon hoped to find."

From that point on excitement mounted in intensity. Each day's work hinted of more discoveries to come. Ruz was now certain that the inspiration for the stairway, the offerings of jade, pearl, human life, and the huge pyramid itself had been one of singular importance to the Maya—thus to archaeological research as well.

The vaulted passageway to which the steps had led them appeared at first to have no further outlet. But a closer examination revealed the presence in the north wall of a triangular-shaped opening blocked by a single stone of herculean proportions. The rubble fill surrounding it was broken open— another vault, enveloped in blackness, lay beyond the wall. Then occurred a drama curiously suggestive of Howard Carter's startling entrance into the burial place of Tutankhamen. The men huddled together in the dimly lighted chamber grew tense with an expectation that only this kind of archaeological high adventure can evoke—the treading back through forgotten civilizations to come suddenly upon splendors unseen for a thousand years or more. A floodlight was beamed into the darkened crypt and Ruz peered through the jagged opening. An instant later he knew his four years of patient labor had been lavishly rewarded. The discovery was of astonishing magnitude. It was some minutes before Ruz could aptly describe the sight confronting him:

"Out of the dim shadows emerged a vision from a fairytale, a fantastic, ethereal sight from another world. It seemed a huge magic grotto carved out of ice, the walls sparkling and glistening like snow crystals. Delicate festoons of stalactites hung like tassels of a curtain, and the stalagmites on the floor looked like the dripping from a great candle. The impression, in fact, was that of an abandoned chapel. Across the walls marched stucco figures in low relief. Then my eye sought the floor. This was almost entirely filled with a great carved stone slab, in perfect condition.

"As I gazed in awe and astonishment, I described the marvelous sight to my colleagues . . . but they wouldn't believe me until they had pushed me aside and had seen with their own eyes the fascinating spectacle. Ours were the first eyes that had gazed on it in more than a thousand years!"

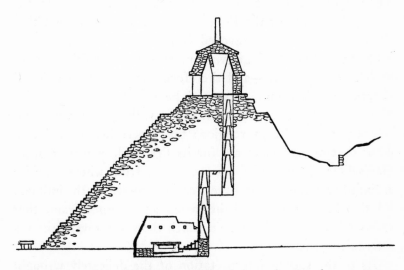

Cross section of the Temple of the Inscriptions, showing the passageway and location of the burial chamber. (*Courtesy Instituto Nacional de Antropología e Historia, Mexico*)

Immediately before him lay the gigantic sculptured stone slab, covering almost half of the chamber's floor space. Its entire surface—slightly more than twelve feet in length by seven in width—was etched in high relief which stood out boldly from its polished surface. In the center was the sensitive figure of a man heavily laden with jewelry and wearing an elaborate headdress, reclining on a thronelike mask. In the center of the tableau stood a large cross, its horizontal arms representing two-headed serpents. Adorning the cross was a lavishly plumed quetzal bird, and bordering the edges of the slab were a series of hieroglyphs pertaining to the sun and moon as well as glyphs denoting Venus and Polaris. Ruz was later able to decipher two calendrical inscriptions corresponding to the years A.D. 603 and 633.

The general design of the monument was strongly reminiscent of that found by Stephens and Catherwood in the nearby Temple of the Cross and another later discovered in the so-called Temple of the Foliated Cross. Ruz points out that these crosslike devices, favored by Palenque's sculptors, were probably symbolic of growing maize—the propitious giver of life to the Maya—and therefore were held in profound veneration. "We may presume," he wrote in the magazine *Archaeology,* in 1953, "that the scene synthesizes fundamental concepts of the Maya religion: the veneration of maize, a plant that needs human aid for its life, and, in turn, assures man's life; the mortal destiny of man, from whose sacrifice springs life in the aspect of the cruciform motif . . . the intimate relation between rain and the farmer; the cosmic frame that surrounds human existence, in which the stars govern the unalterable course of time."

As to the specific interpretation of the delicately wrought motif, Ruz concluded elsewhere that it might well symbolize "the yearning of man for an afterlife. One can't be sure whether the figure depicts mortal man in general or a specific individual for whom the monument was built. He is doomed by fate to be swallowed by the earth, on which he reclines. But in the hope of eternal life he gazes fervently at the cross, the symbol of corn and therefore of life itself."

The slab was contained in a large chamber roughly thirteen feet wide by thirty feet long. Its steeply vaulted ceiling reached to a height of twenty-two feet and was reinforced by five ponderous stones placed as buttresses against the weight of the roof. The phantasmic aspect of the stalactites had resulted from lime deposits issuing from the walls and ceiling, amassing through the centuries into eerie, glistening spires. Adorning the walls were nine human figures, superbly molded in stucco relief and representing the Lords of the Underworld. For more than ten centuries the ornate gods—peering out from a curtain of white stalactites—had guarded the walls of the chamber. Had they been placed there to witness rituals enacted by solemn-faced priests, rites too sacred to perform before the multitudes? Or were they overseers of some secret as yet undisclosed within the vault? The Indians who assisted Ruz in his efforts to reclaim the temple from obscurity knew nothing of Palenque's builders; even legend made no mention of the events that occurred here—the once magnificent city had fallen to ruins long before the first European set foot in the New World.

After several days the ponderous triangular door of the vault was opened. "I entered the mysterious chamber," recalled Ruz, "with the strange sensation natural for the first one to tread the entrance steps in a thousand years. I tried to see it all with the same vision that the Palenque priests had when they left the crypt; I wanted to efface the centuries and hear the vibrations of the last human voices beneath those massive vaults; I strove to capture the cryptic message that those men of old had given us so inviolate. Across the impenetrable veil of time I sought the impossible bond between their lives and ours."

Upon closer examination it was discovered that the sculptured slab covering the floor of the crypt was resting on an immense stone block, which in turn was supported by six rectangular pieces of cut stone. It was an elaborate arrangement obviously designed by skilled craftsmen who understood well the importance of their labors. A suspicion had awakened in Ruz' mind that this gigantic supporting block might well contain the solution to the original purpose of the hidden chamber. To test his inclination it was first necessary to ascertain whether or not it was solid. Its thickness made soundings useless, but by drilling a hole into one side it was soon disclosed that the huge stone was actually a hollow basin. The carved slab above it would have to be raised!

Utilizing the only equipment at his disposal, Ruz devised the idea of placing jacks under each corner of the five-ton cover stone, supported by logs to afford additional leverage. Slowly the immense weight was lifted. It was of utmost importance not to crack or scar the masterpiece they were prying from its base. A feeling of almost unbearable apprehension settled over the faintly lighted crypt.

Ruz recalled that "... as the slab was lifted, inch by inch, we were surprised to find that a smaller inside cover lay below it. Also of stone and smoothly finished, the inner cover was about seven feet long and thirty inches wide. It was of a peculiar curved outline, with one end flared like a fishtail. And at either end was a pair of round holes, fitted with stone plugs exactly like those we had found in the temple floor far above us. By now we knew that these were lifting holes.

"We worked on, breathless with excitement. Every time we jacked the great carved top up an inch we slipped a section of board under it so that, if a jack slipped, the massive sculpture would not fall. When we had raised it about fifteen inches, my curiosity got the best of me."

Ruz squeezed his way under the slab and removed the stone plugs from the inner cover. Through the tiny openings he was able barely to distinguish the contents of the basin.

My first impression was that of a mosaic of green, red, and white. Then it resolved itself into details—green jade ornaments, red painted teeth and bones, and fragments of a mask. I was gazing at the death face of him for whom all this stupendous work—the crypt, the sculpture, the stairway, the great pyramid with its crowning temple—had been built.... This, then, was a sarcophagus, the first ever found in a Mayan pyramid.

After that glimpse it didn't take us long, with ropes through the holes, to get that queer-shaped, rather thin stone cover off, and there the great man was, laid out full length, at the bottom of the deep stone basin, the interior of which had been painted red. Although the bones were so decayed and fragile that we could not make precise measurements to determine his physical type ... he appeared to have been a robust man of forty or fifty, and of good height —about five feet eight inches.... His teeth, although painted red, were normal and were not inset or filled, which was unusual for an adult Maya of high rank.

The great man—he was probably a priest—had no gold ornaments, but here were quantities of jade objects—beads, rings on every finger, bracelets, ear ornaments, and exquisitely carved figurines. These were in the form of flowers, little gourds, bats, snake heads, and human figures with the characteristics of certain Mayan gods. The buried man had a jade ornament in each hand and another in his mouth; his neck and shoulders were covered with a huge collar-and-breast ornament of jade beads. On his face were the remnants of a mask of jade mosaic.... The eyes of the mask were of shell, with inlaid bits of obsidian to form the iris. The only other ornament not of jade was what at first seemed to be an enormous pearl an inch and a half long. This turned out to be several curved pieces of mother of pearl cleverly fitted and glued together....

Having at last discovered the ultimate purpose to which the chamber had been put—that of the burial place of a high priest —the succession of puzzling enigmas encountered by Ruz during his excavations began to make sense. In a manner befitting the pharaohs of Egypt, the preparation of the tomb had assumed the proportions of a full-scale communal effort. It had required years to complete. As it would have been impossible to transport the immense sarcophagus and its carved lid down the finished stairway, the grave had obviously been prepared in advance, and the pyramid supporting the Temple of the Inscriptions was constructed over it.

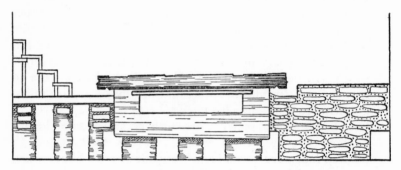

Cross section of the burial chamber with sculptured lid in position over the sarcophagus. (*Courtesy Instituto Nacional de Antropología e Historia, Mexico*)

Relentlessly the populace had carried out their ordained task. Tons of limestone were quarried into huge blocks and rolled on logs to the site. There they were cut into smaller sections and raised into place on the slowly mounting sides of the structure. While the building was in progress, sculptors prepared the stucco reliefs that embellished the temple's façade and the carved stones for its latticed roof comb.

One question in particular puzzled Ruz in his attempt to reconstruct the preceding events: Had the high priest for whom this prodigious outpouring of energy was intended actually supervised the construction of the tomb during his lifetime? Or, rather, was it an act of homage conceived after his death? A possible clue lay in the inclusion of the stairway leading to the burial vault which seemed to indicate that the tomb was intended to remain open until the time of the holy man's funeral.

Ultimately the long planned-for day came to pass. The death of one so revered must indeed have presaged a singular occasion. Unfortunately there is no record of the event. We are left to speculate on its solemnity, to imagine the crowds of peasants gathered at the foot of the temple to leave offerings in homage of the departed priest. Perhaps they had known for some days that his death was near at hand. Sorcerers may have cast piles of corn or *pito* beans on the ground and read into their patterns an omen of misfortune. Or medicine priests attending the ailing man had proclaimed his passing days beforehand. Yet grief was no less heavy upon the populace.

On the prescribed day, the body—swathed in jaguar-skin robes and festooned with jade—was borne down the stairway to the burial chamber by a procession of priests. Their graven faces were painted with sacred symbols; they wore elaborate helmets bedecked with jade and quetzal feathers which cast distorted shadows along the torchlighted walls. Nobles followed closely behind the funerary cortege, accompanying the six youths whose spirits were to guard the entrance to the crypt. A droning chant sounded above the shuffling of sandaled feet, and there were prayers spoken in barely audible murmurs. The descent toward death was long and terror-filled. Their prayer was: "May the grace of the Lords of the Underworld make it otherwise for the honored one who now embarks."

When the procession had entered the burial chamber, the body was lowered into the sarcophagus and the death offerings arranged around it. The holy man's eyes were closed beneath the jade mosaic mask. The inner cover was carefully fitted over the coffin, and the massive sculptured slab was lowered into place above it. Two magnificent human heads—molded of stucco and broken from their original bases—were placed under the sarcophagus as offerings. A jade mosaic and a necklace of polished slate pendants were laid on the sculptured slab above the maize cross. Rubble and stones were then piled around the sarcophagus and the chamber was sealed by sliding the triangular stone door into place in the wall.

Palenque, Chiapas

In the corridor just outside the burial vault the six youths were sacrificed—struck down from behind or strangled in a manner considered propitious for such an occasion. Their limp bodies were packed into the stone coffin and covered with a layer of mortared rubble, exactly as Ruz had found them. Only in times of urgent common need was human sacrifice practiced during the Classic period. A more reckless fondness of the gods for human life was a sacrament disseminated among the Maya by intruders from the Mexican plateau after A.D. 900. It was then that wholesale slaughter was construed as a prime requisite of divine favor. But in Classic times the dedication of six humans—even to insure the eternal fortunes of a powerful priest—was perhaps an extravagant display of adoration.

The memory of the high priest was not allowed to fade with the passing of time. For the living Maya it was desirable to maintain a link with his still-hovering spirit, so the curious stone duct that Ruz had encountered along the wall of the stairway was constructed to serve this purpose. Beginning at the side of the sarcophagus in the form of a carved serpent's head, it extended through the adjacent corridor and along the full length of the stairway to the floor of the temple. Through this open tube passed the incantations of living priests to the dead man below, and perhaps some darkly mysterious confirmation of their acceptance in return. Ruz termed the extraordinary device a "physic duct"—a direct line, as it were, between the living and the unknown realm of death.

It cannot be said with certainty exactly when the stairway leading to the burial chamber was filled with debris and closed. At first it seemed likely that it had been a preordained act to insure the tomb against any immediate threat of desecration. However, Ruz cites the fact that recent excavations have produced evidence that Palenque may have been subjected to a strong wave of outside influence near the close of the ninth century. Hence there is reason to suspect that the tomb—certainly the most important religious shrine within the city—was sealed only as a precaution against the mounting presence of unsympathetic elements.

Details such as these may never be fully clarified. They are among the areas of conjecture that archaeologists can only hope to bridge with intelligent speculation. On the other hand, Ruz' discovery provided extraordinary inroads to more abstract fields of knowledge.

For example, the structural complexity of the Temple of the Inscriptions—with its subterranean stairway, burial vault, and "physic duct"—offers perhaps the most convincing evidence yet discovered of the incredible skill of Mayan architects. It remains a building without equal among the monuments of pre-Columbian civilizations. Its design is wholly unique; its very inspiration forces allowances in the long-established belief that the motivation of pyramid building in Middle America was solely for the purpose of elevating temples. Such was simply not the case at Palenque, and it is highly probable that similar structures await discovery elsewhere.

Also inherent in Ruz' findings were further indications of the power of the priesthoods and the complexity of the society over which they ruled. That the veneration of a single priest could have inspired such a mammoth concentration of effort—engineers, artisans, stonemasons, and peasants working unceasingly over a period of years to construct his tomb—is in itself a poignant measure of the people's subjugation to religious mandates. Yet in retrospect it was but one link in the centuries-long wave of feverish activity that brought dozens of expansive ceremonial centers into existence.

So much concerning Palenque's history remains—as does the entire Mayan problem—in a state of suspension. Like the eloquent city at the steps of the Tumbála Hills, few major sites have been more than partially excavated. Greater still are the dozens of ruins lying virtually unexplored in the illimitable wilderness that was once the Mayan empire.

Nonetheless, a single discovery such as that Alberto Ruz had revealed will often provide archaeologists with a prodigious amount of information in a relatively short time, especially concerning broader aspects of a civilization under study. It is largely a matter of luck: the explorer is as likely to stumble upon the remains of an isolated fortress as those of a major center of political, cultural, or religious occurrences. In entering upon his exploration of the Temple of the Inscriptions, Ruz had been fortunate indeed.

CHAPTER 9

Bonampak: The Mirror of a Golden Age

HAD John Lloyd Stephens ventured a short distance east of Palenque—into the expansive wilderness of the Chiapas rain forests—he would have encountered a curious circumstance: descendants of the ancient Maya whose mode of existence was almost totally unchanged from that of pre-Conquest times. As it happened, Stephens disregarded the vague rumors of their whereabouts in his determination to explore the ruins of Palenque.

Perhaps it was just as well. The assiduous student of antiquities would not have been welcomed in the remote villages of these people known as the Lacandónes. Long before, they had sought the forested depths of Chiapas and Guatemala to escape punitive attempts on the part of the Spanish. Their total isolation stood as a barrier against the further encroachment of outside influences before which they refused to yield. Seclusion had offered their only hope of survival. It was jealously guarded. For almost half a century following Stephens' journey to Palenque, their existence was to remain little more than hearsay.

Alfred Maudslay was considerably more intrigued with the prospect of seeking out and observing the Lacandónes. In the course of his explorations late in the nineteenth century, he was aware that a tribe directly descended from the ancient Maya—

perhaps still preserving their aboriginal way of life—offered a unique opportunity for comparative study.

Maudslay's investigations opened a singularly fascinating field for speculation. Were the furtive Lacandónes the still-pure offspring of the once-illustrious Mayan empire—a people reduced to primeval simplicity in the aftermath of the catastrophic occurrences that brought ruin to the incredible accomplishments of their forebears? And, of even greater significance to scholarly inquiry, had they remained untouched by colonization and conversion during the centuries after the Conquest? If these suppositions were borne out, their study would provide an invaluable conjecture between the present and the archaeological past. A new dimension would be added in retracing the history of the Maya.

Maudslay was intent upon subjecting these queries to closer examination, but his efforts were hampered by the Lacandónes' distrust of intruders and their unwillingness to communicate knowledge of their ways and beliefs. Except for an occasional chance meeting, they remained stealthily hidden in the forest. Even from cursory observations, however, Maudslay was convinced that striking affinities did actually exist between these living inhabitants of the region and the builders of its numerous ancient cities. The Indians encountered during his explorations bore an unmistakable resemblance to the countenances reflected in the sculpture monuments at nearby archaeological sites. Elsewhere among the ruins, notably at Yaxchilán, he discovered religious objects that had recently been left there by visiting tribesmen—small clay idols and crudely fashioned pottery vessels in which copal incense had been burned.

"In nearly all of the houses," wrote Maudslay, "I found earthen pots, partly filled with some half-resinous substance. . . . Some looked newer than others, and many were in such positions that it was clear that they had been placed there since the partial destruction of the houses. I have little doubt that they have been made and brought by the Lacandón Indians. . . ."

At the turn of the century the forested interior of Chiapas—so long desolate and worthless—was opened to economic exploitation by chicle gatherers and woodsmen who discovered lucrative sources of natural gum and mahogany in its remote depths. Occasionally these intruders intermarried with Lacandón women; more often they left behind illegitimate children of mixed blood. Disease and frequent desertion in search of employment and improved conditions have sharply reduced their numbers in recent years. Eventual extinction seems the inevitable consequence of their plight: at present there are approximately one hundred and sixty Lacandónes whose condition holds little promise of a sustained increase.

Among this diminishing population the struggle for survival against the mounting threat of disease and the infiltration of outside influences has confined them to a daily existence of the barest simplicity. Their environment is perhaps the most inhospitable to be found anywhere in Middle America—infinite expanses of humid rain forest infested with malaria-bearing mosquitoes. In its most inaccessible depths are situated their widely scattered settlements consisting of thatched dwellings, usually with open sides allowing infrequent jungle breezes to circulate freely. A single family may live in complete isolation miles from their nearest neighbor; more frequently several families join together and erect clusters of houses arranged around an open plaza which are called *caribals*.

As in times past, maize, planted with crude digging sticks in open milpas, remains the primary basis of their diet, supplemented by tomatoes, beans, squash, cassava, bananas, and papaya. After several seasons the productivity of the milpas becomes exhausted and it is necessary to prepare new fields in repetition of the precarious agricultural cycle upon which Mayan civilization rested at the height of its virility.

Until recent years the Lacandónes depended solely upon their skill in working with natural materials to supply their needs. Cloth was pounded from bark or woven of native cotton on simple looms, the hammocks in which they sleep were fashioned of vegetable fiber. Baskets and trays were made from twigs lashed with yucca fiber. Hollowed gourds and a variety of pottery vessels served to carry water and store foodstuffs. At present many of these handicrafts are being replaced by commercially produced goods acquired by trade.

Both the men and women dress in simple cotton mantles which hang freely without belts or sashes. Occasionally the women of certain groups coil their hair into tight braids bedizened with colored feathers. Usually, however, like the men who are disarmingly fierce in appearance, they allow it to grow uncombed and tangled. A scant few, living in close proximity to populous areas, have reportedly cut their hair as a symbol of their renunciation of tribal customs. So far such occurrences are uncommon.

Following Maudslay's initial observations, no scholarly inroads were made upon the Lacandónes until 1902. It was then that the distinguished anthropologist Alfred M. Tozzer began an exhaustive study which provided the basis for virtually all subsequent inquiries. For two years he lived among various groups, recording a prodigious amount of ethnological data pertaining to their daily life and traditions. Tozzer shared Maudslay's curiosity regarding the existing ties between these people and the ancient Maya, and he patiently sought out every fragment of information, however obscure, which might define unbroken lines of cultural descent.

Such evidence was not readily apparent. There was nothing in the Lacandónes' primitive mode of existence that openly suggested their eloquent heritage. Vanished was the knowledge of astronomy, mathematics, hieroglyphs, architecture, and sculpture which elevated their forebears to irrecoverable levels of attainment. Lost beyond remembrance were the tutelar deities of the Mayan pantheon, the myths and legends of their intractable wanderings on earth. Obscured was their conscious lineage with the builders of the fallen cities scattered through their domain, except for a vague awareness of the miracle of their splendor, a whispered veneration for the "ancient ones."

But there were other unmistakable indications that the Lacandónes recognized a closer affinity with the Maya than they were willing to confirm. Aside from the matter of their obvious physical resemblance to figures depicted in Mayan sculptural art, Tozzer was of the opinion that their language had changed very little from that spoken by the Maya centuries before.

In their religion, too, analogies with the past were to be found. Sylvanus Morley made the interesting observation that the religious practices of the Lacandónes closely parallel those of the ancient Maya as they probably existed before organized priesthoods brought about their severe formalization: there were no hierarchies, no complex rituals or elaborate places of worship. The heads of families served as priests, overseeing rites carried out within crude shrines dedicated to a simple form of nature worship that imparted living personification to all the elements of natural environment; clouds, air, rocks, animals, rivers, and stars—in short, everything—were believed to be equally alive with mankind. Foot races determined whose strength was greater than that of the wind; a mountain was climbed to conquer its spirit; when an animal was slain, its forgiveness was fervently sought. And rough images of stone and clay gave tangible form to supernatural beings. Such had very likely been the tenor of archaic Mayan religion. It closely approximated the practices extant among the Lacandónes.

Within open thatched-roof shelters rituals are enacted before crude altars containing rows of earthen images and curious vessels known as "god pots." These ceramic bowls, decorated with effigy representations of spirits, are the focal point of their rites: balls of resinous copal incense are burned inside them and prayers recited while they smolder. Copal has always figured prominently in Mayan ritualism, and there is positive archaeological evidence linking this method of Lacandón worship with similar ancient practices.

On occasion the Lacandónes seek to heighten the intensity of religious experiences by drinking excessively of a liquor known as *baltche*. It is brewed from the bark of the *baltche* tree fermented with corn and wild honey. The result is an intoxicant intended to bring those who partake of it into closer communion with the gods. Its consumption was widely practiced by the early Maya, and the formula has remained unaltered for centuries.

At specific intervals pilgrimages journey to the densely over-grown city of Yaxchilán where, it is thought, still powerful Mayan deities hover among the crumbled buildings. Its deserted temples become the scene of ceremonials enacted in guarded secrecy. God pots are placed at various shrines, and prayers offered amid veils of copal smoke. Meager offerings of maize and copal are left behind on crumbled altars that once received the treasures of a grandiose empire. Momentarily the white-robed Lacandónes emerge from their sylvan existence to stand awed in the shadows of a plundered heritage; to enter temples no longer accustomed to human voices; pray before effaced, nameless gods; look upon carvings of priests and nobles whose profiles are identically mirrored in their own; to recapture something of the venerable legacy exchanged during the desperate pursuit of seclusion that carried them steadily farther from the intellectual precocity they had sought to preserve. Actuality dimmed into faint recollection, and that in turn into memorial oblivion. The exigencies of momentary survival permitted the accomplishments of a thousand years to slip from their hands. A regressive tide swept them back beyond the dim shadows of exalted priesthoods, templed cities, and pristine artistry to the bleak shores of Archaic existence. And there they have remained—an example of the mutations inflicted by history upon its progeny.

Bonampak, Chiapas

In the spring of 1946 an explorer-photographer named Giles G. Healey entered the desolate frontiers of northern Chiapas. He had been commissioned to produce a documentary film on the history of the Maya from pre-Columbian times to the present day. His mission on this particular journey was to photograph the scarcely known Lacandónes.

While working among a group who occupied the densely forested bottomlands of the Lacanjá River, Healey noticed that small numbers of men would disappear from the village for several days at a time, reportedly to take part in pilgrimages to shrines forbidden to the eyes of outsiders. Healey's curiosity was fervently aroused. He was well aware that the area abounded with archaeological remains; but the prospect, however remote, of visiting a site still venerated by living descendants of its builders offered an irresistible challenge.

Eventually Healey succeeded in bargaining for the whereabouts of the hidden shrine. He was guided deep into the surrounding forest. In places hardly a shaft of sunlight penetrated the overhanging bush; one could easily have passed within a few yards of an entire city without remotely suspecting its existence. Finally they emerged into a less thickly wooded area enclosed by shrouded masses of white stone. Before them were the visible remains of eight structures resting on what had once been a terraced acropolis.

Although scarcely distinguishable beneath a dense vesture of underbrush, the buildings were low, rectangular, and of stark simplicity. Some were partially buried in debris; others stood almost as they had been abandoned—like chalk-white phantoms rising out of a sea of jungle green.

In a great sunken plaza at the foot of the acropolis lay a massive sculptured stela. Its figuration was that of a lavishly bejeweled priest holding a ceremonial staff surrounded by hieroglyphic inscriptions. Flanking a stairway that ascended the acropolis were two more elaborately carved stelae half buried in the earth. Other monuments—figures of jaguars and coiled serpents—were scattered about the jungle floor. Healey was now close to a disclosure of sensational aspect and profound importance!

The largest of the buildings stood near the northern slope of the acropolis. Despite trees growing from its roof, it had remained in a remarkably good state of preservation. Three doors opened into a series of interior vaults, and sculptured figures had formerly adorned its façade above each entrance. A single badly eroded fragment of stucco relief was still discernible on the outer wall between the second and third doorways.

Healey passed through one of the entrances and entered a narrow, steeply vaulted room. As his eyes adjusted to the chamber's faint illumination, he was suddenly aware of countless faces peering at him from the walls and ceiling. A moment later they had assumed sharp delineation and colors faintly muted by age. He was surrounded by processions of lavishly costumed priests and nobles, attended by servants and warriors. Entering the next room, he came upon a tableau of opposing armies locked in battle—brown-skinned warriors entangled in confused attitudes of combat. Still more figures—dancers in wildly exotic costumes—covered the walls of the third room. What Healey had stumbled upon was actually a dazzling array of murals completely covering the walls of the temple's three interior chambers.

It was obvious that it would be necessary to return properly equipped to photograph the superb murals, bringing with him specialists to assess their archaeological value. Unknown to Healey at the time of his initial visit, the existence of these particular ruins had been reported only four months earlier by two American travelers, John G. Bourne and Carl Frey. Bourne had actually drawn detailed plans of the standing buildings, but so thick was the veil of jungle that they had completely overlooked the structure containing the frescoes.

The following year, in the winter of 1947, Healey led an expedition jointly sponsored by the United Fruit Company, the Carnegie Institution, and the Mexican government back to the obscured site. He was accompanied by two artists experienced in mural restoration—António Tejeda and Agustín Villagra Caleti—who set about a challenging project of copying the paintings in accurate detail. The site was assigned the name Bonampak—a Mayan phrase meaning "painted walls."

From air strips at the remote outposts of El Cedro, Filadelfia, or Tenosique on the banks of the Usumacinta River, a journey of several days by mule along hazardous trails is required to reach the densely overgrown buildings, which each year cloak themselves in a fresh canopy of underbrush. Despite its extreme difficulty of access, numerous expeditions have sought to probe deeper into Bonampak's history and evaluate its astounding artistic attainments. Art and archaeology are normally closely allied, yet few discoveries have evoked the mutual interest of scientists and art historians to the degree of intensity as did Bonampak.

Oddly enough, it had apparently been a city of minor importance. It was one of numerous small centers that flourished in the Usumacinta Valley between A.D. 400 and 900, receiving political and cultural impetus from nearby Palenque, Yaxchilán, and Piedras Negras.

Apparently Bonampak's artists had drawn for inspiration and basic techniques of execution upon traditions long established in these larger cities, especially at Yaxchilán. The eminent scholar of Mayan sculpture, Tatiana Proskouriakoff, writes that Bonampak "could not have been more than a small center in a region crowded with other towns. It was without doubt merely a dependency of the much larger city of Yaxchilán. The stamp of the Yaxchilán style in its works of art is unmistakable, and the artists who for a generation gave Bonampak its singular distinction were probably trained in the schools of the larger city."

Why Bonampak should have been graced with the most eminent artistic attainment of its day we shall perhaps never know. Without considering for a moment the incredible ingenuity of its muralists, Bonampak's sculptural art ranks among the finest examples thus far discovered. Proskouriakoff described the immense stela found in the city's main plaza as "one of the largest and finest monuments ever set up by the Maya." Its other examples of stone sculpture, although few in number, are hardly less superb in concept and workmanship. And when the murals were finally executed, an already profound mastery of expression was brought to an unparalleled climax.

Numerous examples of pre-Columbian mural art have survived at widely scattered sites throughout Mexico and Central America. Ornate painted frescoes were uncovered on the walls of tombs at Monte Albán in Oaxaca, and at Teotihuacán in the Valley of Mexico. Interesting specimens have also been found at Uaxactún, Palenque, Chacmultun, and Tulum, in the Mayan area. Exceptionally well-executed murals came to light in the

Temple of the Warriors and the Temple of the Jaguars at Chichén Itzá in Yucatán. Yet students of pre-Columbian art take note of the fact that these were of radically different tenor than the frescoes of Bonampak. Usually, as Proskouriakoff points out, they were designed to convey extremely abstract symbolism in keeping with their ritualistic or mythological sources of inspiration. Except for a few examples of Mayan painting—notably the murals at Chichén Itzá which depict scenes of battle—realism in pre-Columbian art was virtually unknown.

Proskouriakoff writes: "Some of the less highly institutionalized cultures expressed life realistically and very successfully by the manufacture of pottery figurines, but the great religious arts were overburdened with esoteric symbols and had little regard for common occurrences. The murals of Teotihuacán no doubt could give us interesting data of the formal aspect of Mexican religion were we able to read their symbols, but their scenes, depicting deities, mythological monsters, and men in fantastic environments, make little comment on real life. We can only appreciate them as decorative patterns and speculate on what they signify. . . . Aside from colorful decorations their chief purpose is symbolic discourse."

Sculpture assumed an even greater degree of formality, for there was much less latitude in the medium of stone. Thus it is essentially true that the great artistic traditions evolved by pre-Columbian civilizations impart to modern scholars little more than images and ideas of ritualistic significance. Art was never used to capture and convey vignettes of daily life—festivals, street scenes, hunting, individual portraits, or the drama of the common man. For this reason the Bonampak murals offered a new dimension in evaluating Mayan artistic achievement: they represent a literal translation into form and color of actual occurrences; here for the first time we encounter Mayan artists venturing far afield into realistic expression.

Varied aspects of their culture—stately processions, cere-monialism, warfare, the judgment of captives and musicians—are vividly portrayed in a style unhampered by occult symbols or florid decorative embellishments. Sylvanus Morley declared that "some of the figures in the Bonampak murals exhibit a de-gree of naturalism which western European art did not achieve until several centuries later." However, Proskouriakoff cau-tions against carrying such comparisons too far toward the Renaissance. Mayan painters, she notes, were unconcerned with perspective, subtleties of coloration, and the illusion of third dimension which dominated Western artistic expression from the Middle Ages forward. Nor did the Maya ever work with other than human and symbolic forms, and always their figures were depicted in strict profile.

"Maya art," writes Proskouriakoff, "in its concentration on rhythmic, expressive line, and its forthright and unpretentious observations comes nearer to realizing the objectives of Orien-tal painting. As compared with Chinese painting, however, it is severely handicapped by its preoccupation with the silhouette, and its neglect of all natural forms except that of the human figure. . . . We miss, therefore, in Maya painting the wonderful skill with which the Chinese transformed mountains into har-monies of rhythm and the minor motions of their lines of drapery. Perhaps, however, these omissions so distinctive of the Maya style should be regarded not as faults but as econ-omies. How much they could express in simple outline is ad-mirable. . . ."

In restoring and copying the murals the artists Tejeda and Caleti encountered formidable technical difficulties. Certain areas were completely obliterated by decay, and the surviving paintings were obscured by a layer of lime deposited over them by seeping water. As it was not possible to clean the walls without damaging the murals, it was necessary to find a sub-stance that would render the deposit transparent and bring out the full brilliance of the underlying colors. After lengthy experimentation it was discovered that the liberal application of kerosene produced the desired effect.

In copying the paintings an attempt was made to retrace the steps by which they had originally been executed. It appeared that the figures had first been drawn with a light red line on the uncolored plaster walls. Flat areas were then filled in with color, and the figures retraced and accentuated with a heavier black outline. Both Tejeda and Caleti believe the original outlines were painted while the wall plaster was still wet, thus achieving a true fresco technique.

Caleti was of the opinion that brushes of animal hair or feathers were used to apply broad areas of color, and rabbit fur served for more exacting detail. The artists had drawn upon an extensive palette of colors extracted from mineral substances. Blue was compounded of crushed beidellite. Reds and pinks were of iron oxide. Yellow was extracted from ocher, dark brown from bitumen or asphalt, and black from carbon. A wide range of greens was obtained by mixing blue and yellow in varying proportions.

Working by the light of torches, on ladders and scaffolds made of lashed poles, the Bonampak muralists had completely covered the walls of the Painted Temple's three interior chambers with profiles of elaborately robed priests and nobles, musicians, armed warriors, captives, and masked dancers marching through a series of related tableaux. Unwittingly, they were at the same time leaving future archaeologists a wealth of otherwise obscure information concealed in minute details of their creations. Hieroglyphic inscriptions indicated that they were painted sometime near the close of the eighth century.

Since their discovery the interpretation of the frescoes has constituted a unique field of study. Here for the first time was a priceless mirror of Mayan life and times. Archaeologists

Bonampak, Chiapas

were able to extract extremely valuable data concerning such details as musical instruments, costumes and dress, methods of warfare, the role of human sacrifice, and the enactment of rituals. Ultimately the difficult task of interpreting the entire sequence of events represented in the murals was undertaken by J. Eric Thompson. Of necessity such reconstructions rest in part upon supposition, for the meaning of numerous details can only be guessed and portions of the murals are permanently obliterated by age. Even so, they have yielded graphic confirmation of much that eluded previous archaeological deduction.

We see depicted on the walls of the first room a grand array of royal personages, including the *halach uinic,* represented in ceremonial attire. Around them dancers, attended by servants, are donning costumes with lavish decorations of quetzal feathers. On a lower panel there appears a group of masked dancers accompanied by musicians bearing rattles, a drum, trumpets, and a whistle.

The frescoes on the south, east, and west walls of the central room portray a raid upon an enemy settlement. Hoards of warriors, their bodies richly painted, have hurled themselves against their opponents with dazzling fury. On the north wall the spoils of the conflict are exhibited: the prisoners (presumably taken for sacrificial purposes) kneel before the victorious

Mayan nobles to await the pronouncement of their fate—
whether slavery or ceremonial execution.

On the walls of the last room the final supplication is enacted
—the moment of supreme communion with the gods climaxed
by the precious gift of human life. The ecstasy of the participants has broken forth in the ebullient color and restless
movements of the richly clad dancers. Amid them is a dead
captive whose hands and feet are held by attendants; a priest
flails his limp body with a wandlike object.

The French anthropologist and diplomat Jacques Soustelle
recently wrote: "Bonampak is a sort of pictorial encyclopaedia
of a Maya city of the eighth century; the city comes to life there
again, with its ceremonies and its processions, its stiff and
solemn-looking dignitaries weighed down by their heavy
plumed adornments, its warriors clothed in jaguar-skins. Lively
or violent scenes are there displayed side by side with gracious,
familiar pictures of daily life. A complete cross-section of society—women, children, servants, musicians, warrior chiefs,
dying prisoners, masked dancers—that is what these painters
of 1300 years ago succeeded in depicting on those walls, lost
today in the depths of one of the continent's most impenetrable
jungles. . . . Only naïve illusion, born of egocentricity, could
permit us to apply the word 'primitivism' to an art carried to
perfection through centuries of effort—an art which, like any
other, was, in its time and place, the supreme creation of a
genuine culture." *

Perhaps it was with a sense of urgency that Bonampak's
artists labored to record the eloquence of their times. Events
throughout the Mayan empire were assuming an ominous restlessness. Proskouriakoff writes of a vague apprehension which
pervaded their sensibilities: "As far as we know, this was the
last brilliant chapter in the history of this region. We see at

* From *Mexico, Pre-Hispanic Paintings*, Vol. X, UNESCO World Art Series.
Courtesy of the New York Graphic Society, Greenwich, Connecticut.

Bonampak its full pomp, its somewhat barbarous and elaborately designed ritual. . . . There is a bare hint, a mere suggestion in the dramatic scenes, and in the excitement of line foreign to the serenity of the Maya style, of an emotional tension which may have presaged a crisis; but there is, unfortunately, no sequel to the scenes. . . ."

The year A.D. 800 was reached: life continued as before in the dozens of cities scattered across the southern highlands or lying secluded in the luxuriant forest of the Petén and the Usumacinta Valley. Yet the Maya were on the brink of a catastrophic upheaval; their magnificent city-states had but a moment longer to live.

CHAPTER 10

The Riddle of a Vanished Empire

FOR all that is not yet known about the Maya, archaeologists have made significant strides toward outlining the major steps in the development of their civilization. The evolution of distinct cultural manifestations from the early formative centuries onward has been defined. Specific styles in art and architecture are identifiable with certain locales and chronological periods, and much concerning their life and times in general has been reconstructed. Above all, the date inscriptions from at least sixty widely scattered cities have now been deciphered and compared. Scholars had long before learned to expect that such hard-won insights into the lineage of dead civilizations often lead to problems of even greater complexity. Now they were confronted with the most baffling enigma thus far encountered.

By the end of the eighth century A.D. the Maya had achieved their highest peak of intellectual and aesthetic attainments. At least twenty major religious centers and dozens of less important ones were flourishing in opulent splendor. Religious and artistic endeavors were fervently pursued, and the priesthoods had swelled in power and number to a position of absolute authority. And each time a new building or monument was erected the date of its dedication was unfailingly inscribed in hieroglyphic texts. It had always been thus: the succession of readable calendric inscriptions extended unbroken from the earliest dated stela at Uaxactún until the apex of Mayan advancement was reached late in the eighth century. But there it stopped! At successive points during the ninth century the practice of raising dated stelae was relinquished throughout the vast regions occupied by the Maya.

As though by voluntary acts of self-dissolution, the endeavors by which their eminence had been achieved came to an abrupt end—suddenly and without motives clearly defined by archaeological evidence. Intellectual pursuits ground to a halt; the elaborate ritualism which had nourished the growth of Mayan culture was seemingly abandoned. Even the computation of time—the guidepost against which all acts and events had been measured—ceased to be important. Incredible though it may seem, the Maya evacuated their long-cherished places of worship, leaving the labor of centuries to the ravages of time.

The temples were emptied of their priestly guardians, copal incense no longer smoldered upon sacred altars within them, voices had ceased to echo from the plazas. Yet the cities were left untouched, without destruction or alteration, as if their inhabitants had expected to return momentarily. But they did not. Instead, an immense stillness enveloped them from which they were never again to awaken. Grass overtook the courtyards, vines and the spreading roots of trees crept into doorways and sought nourishment in the lime mortar between the stones of pyramids and temples, forcing them to part and crumble. Within a century the jungle had reclaimed the ill-destined cities of the Maya. That an energetic empire should have been totally forsaken at the very height of its glory is a phenomenon without historical parallel. It was, as Stephens had once reflected, "a mourning witness to the world's mutations."

Scholars were puzzled by the lack of evidence pointing to circumstances which could satisfactorily explain a catastrophe of such magnitude: a vast geographical area—teeming with the most vigorous, highly advanced peoples in Middle America —left bare, given up to ruin within the span of a century. Events such as these had to be rooted in factual occurrences which could be retraced by some thread of evidence however obscure it might appear.

At the time the Maya were achieving their maximum expansion—from the fifth century onward—the territories immediately above and below their secluded realm were witnessing equally intensive activity on the part of other civilized groups. Along the frontiers of Chiapas and Tabasco, they came into close contact with various peoples from the direction of the Mexican mainland. Eventually routes of trade were established between the Maya and these neighboring tribes. Excavations have indicated that manifestations derived from the Mexican plateau were present, especially in the southern highlands, at a very early date.

Was it conceivable that the prosperous empire of the Maya had eventually lured conquering armies from among Mexico's less peaceful tribes? Had they succeeded in overpowering and plundering the resplendent cities in their path of conquest? It was a distinct possibility, but one which subsequently failed to enlist archaeological evidence in its behalf. The obvious ravages of warfare were not imprinted upon the ruins. Walls were not found that appear to have been battered in by force, no weapons were scattered about in streets and courtyards, nor the awkward remains of warriors whose death struggle might have driven the inhabitants from the cities in fear of their lives. No such story was contained in the earth removed by the shovels of archaeologists.

Other widely divergent theories were advanced to explain what had become a mystery without equal among students of American prehistory. It was suggested that a sudden metamorphosis in climatic conditions may have deluged the Mayan area with disastrous amounts of rainfall; or that earthquakes had shaken some cities from their foundations, causing others to be abandoned in fear that the disaster might recur. Outbreaks of yellow fever and malaria were cited as still another motive for the sudden exodus. But none of these explanations —based as they were upon hypothetical suppositions—have drawn convincing support from archaeological findings. Silence continued to enshroud the fate of the Maya; scholars were compelled to look elsewhere for an answer to the riddle.

Sylvanus Morley—one of the foremost Mayan experts of the last half-century—directed a considerable amount of research toward this particular problem. As its solution had not been found by attributing the collapse of the Old Empire to external calamities, either by human or natural causes, he sought a motive within the framework of Mayan culture itself —social degeneration, civil strife, or economic failure. But what might have presaged a sudden internal crisis of such far-reaching consequences? For Morley and a number of his colleagues, the answer was bound up in the theory of "agricultural exhaustion"—the belief that the Mayan system of farming, which had remained appallingly primitive since its inception, simply could not produce enough food to sustain an expanding population. In *The Ancient Maya* Morley wrote: *

> The repeated clearing and burning of ever-increasing areas of forest to serve as corn lands gradually converted the original forest into man-made grasslands, artificial savannas. When this process was complete . . . when the primeval forest had been largely felled and replaced in time by these artificially produced grasslands, then agriculture as practiced by the ancient Maya came to an end, since they had no implements whatsoever for turning the soil— no hoes, picks, harrows, spades, shovels, or plows.
> The replacing of the original forest by man-made savan-

---

* Reprinted from *The Ancient Maya,* by Sylvanus G. Morley, with the permission of the publishers, Stanford University Press. Copyright 1946, 1947, and 1956 by the Board of Trustees of Leland Stanford Junior University.

nas ... must have come about very gradually, reaching a
really acute state at different cities and eventually causing
their respective abandonments at different times, depending
in each case upon variable factors such as relative sizes of
the population in question, respective periods of occupation,
and general fertility of the surrounding areas.

Other adverse factors following in the wake of the de-
creasing food supply, such as accompanying social unrest,
governmental disorganization, even religious disbelief,
doubtless all played their respective parts in the collapse ...
but it appears highly probable that economic failure—the
law of diminishing returns, another way of saying the high
cost of living—was chiefly responsible for the final disinte-
gration of the Mayan Old Empire.

If Morley's assumption was correct, then Mayan civilization, with its astounding ingenuity in other fields of endeavor,
had floundered and crumbled for lack of certain implements
which were incident to the rudest beginnings of agriculture elsewhere in the ancient world. Ironically it would then have been
great seas of grass—not sweeping plagues, catastrophic upheavals, or invading armies—that were responsible for top-
pling the Mayan empire.

It was a plausible theory: the crude digging sticks of Mayan
farmers could offer no resistance to a tightly grown net of
jungle grass covering their fields, and the endless quest of new
lands would have carried them steadily farther from the cities,
eventually forcing their abandonment in the wake of mass
migrations of their inhabitants to distant areas.

But did the Maya actually exhaust their vast reserves of un-
cultivated land? It was a difficult conclusion for many scholars
to reconcile in view of subsequent evidence to the contrary. For
instance, an analysis by the eminent archaeologist A. V. Kidder
demonstrated that the soil of the Motugua Valley in Honduras,
once thickly populated by the Maya, is annually revitalized by
flooding. Thus instead of lying fallow for long periods of time,

during which it might have been enveloped by grass, it was probably farmed continually. Elsewhere in regions such as the Petén lowlands, where no such obvious process of fertilization occurred, J. Eric Thompson has observed that vacant lands immediately revert to forest rather than grass savannas. Nor

Tikal

was it entirely plausible that the depletion of land throughout the immense and varied geographical environs occupied by the Maya at the height of their florescence would have necessitated the sudden abandonment of their far-flung centers almost precisely within the span of a century. Kidder pointed out that the Petén region was as densely populated at the outset of the Classic period as it was in the ninth century, yet its inhabitants flourished there for some six centuries with no apparent signs of economic strain. Indications are that the desertion of the cities came about abruptly as though presaged by some event less predictable than the gradual wearing out of their milpas. Judging by the termination of dated stelae, the process of abandonment was under way by A.D. 800. Shortly thereafter, Copán was surrendered to the forest from which Stephens was to reclaim its forgotten splendors. Gradually it spread through the central lowlands until it plundered the heavily populated centers of the northern Yucatán Peninsula early in the tenth century. In its wake the major achievements of Mayan civilization lay in ruins!

Archaeologists were now dealing with questions of far-reaching consequences; in effect they were undertaking a grand-scale autopsy to determine the cause of death of an entire civilization. As inevitably happens, other horizons of conjecture were suggested by the disclosure of previously unknown facts.

Along the waters of the Usumacinta River a city known as Piedras Negras lies deeply buried in the rain forest. Its ruins have yielded a number of sculptured monuments which rank among the finest ever wrought by Mayan artisans. One such piece was a beautifully carved dais originally erected to serve as a "throne" for priests of high rank. From its condition it appeared to have been intentionally smashed, although the exact date of its destruction could not be ascertained. Elsewhere at Piedras Negras a second work of exquisite craftsmanship was unearthed—a sculptured wall panel depicting a high priest presiding over a hierarchic conclave. Again its damaged condition could not logically be accounted for by natural causes —the heads of each of its fifteen individual figures had been knocked off, leaving sharp breaks in the stone.

Excavations at Tikal by the University of Pennsylvania Museum have recovered several stelae which evidence purposeful defacement in a manner similar to the monuments at Piedras Negras. The most important such discovery—a superbly carved monument known as Stela 26—had been shattered and placed upside down in a pile of rubble. From accompanying indications there could be little question that the monolith's defacement occurred sometime *before* Tikal was abandoned. The potential significance of this evidence was noted with heightening interest: the willful destruction of objects intimately associated with long-established religious practices, objects which for centuries had been the cherished reflections of an unquestioned faith. Did not their deliberate destruction

—providing it had occurred in each case prior to the abandonment of the cities in question—indicate the presence of forces
in defiance of the priesthoods at whose direction they had originally been erected? And remembering that the primary function of the cities had been as centers of religious activity and
the dwelling places of the priests, was it not possible that such
manifestations bore witness to an eventual uprising of the
peasant population against their theocratic overlords, resulting
either in the desertion of religious shrines or an acute decline
in their importance?

A growing number of archaeologists began to explore this
possibility as the long-sought resolution of the dramatic happenings that signaled the demise of the Old Empire. J. Alden
Mason, writing in a bulletin of the University of Pennsylvania
Museum, stated that the most likely explanation of the enigma
"is the same as that which caused the downfall of the later
Mayan cities in Yucatán, as well as of most of the great civilizations of antiquity in the Old World, warfare and civil strife.
Probably the people, weary of the yoke of the priesthood, with
their interminable demands for building and ceremonies, revolted. At Piedras Negras, at any rate, the archaeological evidence definitely indicates that the ceremonial furnishings were
intentionally damaged, the monuments mutilated, and its ceremonial center abandoned."

As this supposition was more deeply probed it became apparent that not only the Maya, but other cultures flourishing
at the same time in Mexico, had in all probability fallen victim
to similar internal disturbances. It was a curious fact that several highly accomplished peoples—among them the Zapotecs
of Oaxaca and the inhabitants of Teotihuacán who dominated
the Valley of Mexico—seem to have lapsed into decline
at about the same time. In each case the underlying factors
appeared to stem initially from weaknesses within the framework of these societies, most probably the oppressive power of

the ruling hierarchies. Indeed, it was a route of inquiry worthy of exhaustive study. George Brainerd, in a recent revision of Morley's *The Ancient Maya,* wrote that "the causal element for the Maya decline may be restricted and defined if we assume that the contemporaneous decline of other Classic New World civilizations were influenced by historically related causes. . . . Just as peoples in widely spaced areas of aboriginal America developed similar formal governments ruled by priests, they may have tired simultaneously of this way of life. The lower classes must have revolted, and word must have traveled. Such a drastic change may well have been caused by the formation of an organized set of new ideas as to the purpose of existence—a new philosophy.

"Whatever caused the fall of the Maya priests it was amazingly complete." *

J. Eric Thompson, one of the first scholars to evaluate these tenets, in his book, *The Rise and Fall of Maya Civilization,* has examined closely the important question of how and why the power of the priesthoods might have been undermined. In his estimation it is far from improbable that the mystical enchantment of their esoteric cults eventually wore thin in the eyes of the overburdened multitudes. Of what value to the common man were strivings into abstract realms of mathematics and astronomy which no longer concerned the simpler gods of the earth and sky—knowledge which was kept from them as sacred beyond their caste and complex beyond their ability to understand? Too long had the masses remained in a state of servitude, too exacting was the burden of labor required to erect temples and tend the fields necessary to support the priestly orders. And too obvious were the tricks with which the priests were weaving their cabalistic patterns of psycholog-

---

* Reprinted from *The Ancient Maya,* by Sylvanus G. Morley, with the permission of the publishers, Stanford University Press. Copyright 1946, 1947, and 1956 by the Board of Trustees of Leland Stanford Junior University.

ical domination—the system of punishments and rewards intended to awe the populace into strict obeyance.

It had not always been so. The priesthoods were rooted in genuinely construed mysticism, an almost desperate quest for understanding of environmental and supernatural phenomena. Out of this had arisen dogma and formalization, until—having charted the heavens, measured the seasons, and designed ritualistic expressions which openly dramatized and thus relieved commonly held fears—the priests had been able to demonstrate their ability to insure the continuation of life.

Before such powers the masses of peasantry had lain prostrate, until the shadows of despotism and degeneracy were glimpsed and the cry arose for rebellion. Swiftly the populace— supported perhaps by warriors, for their trust as well had been abused—overturned the authority of the priests. Whether they were banished or slaughtered outright may never be fully ascertained, but the cities—the surviving symbols of their reign— were thereafter abandoned to ruin.

Elsewhere in history a people in revolt against oppressive overlords was an often-repeated circumstance. Its application to the Maya—allowing for digressions inherent in their unique social and religious structure—may very well be the key to the mysterious circumstances underlying the fall of the city-states!

As yet there is no one among contemporary Mayan scholars who insists upon the unqualified acceptance of any one solution underlying the collapse of the Classic period. Existing evidence is far too fragmentary. And with immense areas of Chiapas and the Yucatán Peninsula—where the events in question mainly occurred—still to be subjected to extensive excavation, absolute conclusions cannot reasonably be inferred.

It might well have been that a conspiracy of differing circumstances lies at the bottom of the enigma. As Morley suggested, agricultural failure in one or two widely scattered locales could easily have presaged a widening loss of faith in

the priesthoods elsewhere. Revolts were thereby touched off
which gained impetus from still other sources of unrest. Had
such been the case, then the idea of "agricultural exhaustion"
and more recent speculations concerning the outbreak of civil
disturbances would very likely have overlapped in cause and
effect.

Whatever the actual reasons that made necessary the abandonment of the once-populous city-states, they were irreconcilable with the destiny of the Maya. The last date inscriptions
recovered so far from cities of the Classic period fall within the
first quarter of the tenth century: by then the process of sur-
rendering their vast empire to the jungle was complete.

For the Maya the Age of Aesthetics was ended—they would
never again attain the intellectual eminence they had nurtured
for almost a thousand years. Yet their history did not terminate
at this sudden juncture. A turning point had been reached, the
inception of a new era, a shift in cultural emphasis and locale.
Archaeologically, the six centuries that now lay between the
failure of the Old Empire and the Spanish Conquest are fashioned of the malcontent restlessness, unreasoned violence, and
political intrigue which prelude oblivion!

CHAPTER 11

Chichén Itzá: The Mecca
of Warrior Gods

WHAT, then, became of the vibrant nucleus of Mayan culture? Had it continued to flounder in the midst of its decaying cities? Had its survivors succumbed to inbreeding and intellectual atrophy which reduced them in time to a state of near savagery? Over Guatemala, Honduras, and the dense interior of Chiapas such had been the case. But the presence of ruins of a different nature in the northern half of the Yucatán Peninsula hinted that vestiges of Mayan civilization had lingered a while longer in the afterglow of its former brilliance.

Scattered across the present Mexican states of Campeche, Quintana Roo, and Yucatán lies a spectacular array of archaeological remains. The chronicles of the conquistadors had spoken of these ruins; the soldiers of Francisco de Montejo had battled hordes of warriors in their very shadows. Clearly they were of Mayan origin, but scholars were uncertain exactly where these sites could be fitted chronologically into the sequence of events in Middle America.

Until recently archaeologists attributed their florescence to the period immediately following the collapse of the Old Empire. It was believed that these centers had been populated by emigrants from the south as early as the fifth century A.D. Along two separate routes they had moved northward in a series of gradual migrations. On the east coast of the peninsula occurred what was termed the "Lesser Descent"—former inhabitants of the Petén area who found their way to the northeastern corner of Yucatán. Across the peninsula, along the west coast, the "Great Descent" brought peoples from the Usumacinta Valley and the southern highlands to settle in northwestern Yucatán, in an area of low, bush-covered outcroppings known as the Puuc Hills. These early migrants established numerous provincial villages, but it was not until the ultimate failure of the Old Empire that its survivors, whose exigent wanderings eventually brought them to northern Yucatán, imparted to these outlying provinces the superior accomplishments of their more advanced heritage.

Here, between the tenth and thirteenth centuries, there was believed to have followed a renaissance of Mayan culture climaxed by the flowering of magnificent ceremonial centers designed after the grand scale of the abandoned cities to the south. Almost simultaneously they had come into existence: Uxmal, Kabah, Sayil, Labná, Izamal, and Chichén Itzá were the largest of many others to be wrought by the experienced hands of the newcomers. Under a modified regime, life assumed its former pattern. The priesthoods took up their ecclesiastic power, the nobility grasped the familiar helm of leadership, and the peasants once more set to work erecting buildings and clearing land for milpas. Thus was born what was known as the New Empire. It was to endure until shortly before the Spanish Conquest!

At the time this hypothesis seemed highly plausible. Relatively little excavation had been carried out in the upper Yucatán Peninsula. Ceramic stratigraphy—which often acts as a yardstick for defining cultural relationships—was not yet clearly established, and the dated monuments recovered from this locale presented an incomplete chronological sequence. Yet the apparent differences between the northern cities and those of the Old Empire were sufficient to convince most scholars that they had been erected *after* Mayan civilization had undergone a complete reorientation from its earlier traditions.

Another fact as well seemed to bear out these speculations. Specific place names in Yucatán are constantly mentioned in the native chronicles written after the Conquest; in each of the surviving accounts they are associated with events of historical importance. References to Chichén Itzá, Uxmal, and a large center known as Mayapán frequently appear in the *Books of Chilam Balam*. Histories compiled by native informants and much of the data drawn upon by Spanish chroniclers concerned the role of these cities in the later years of Mayan history. Although they were abandoned at the time of the Conquest, recollections of events which had supposedly occurred within them were still vividly implanted in the folklore of the region. To the older Classic cities—which by then lay totally in ruins—there are no references whatsoever in historic documents. So the pronouncement that Chichén Itzá, Uxmal, and the numerous other ruins scattered across the northern half of the Yucatán Peninsula represented the rebirth of Mayan culture at the hands of emigrants from the Old Empire seemed reasonably justified both by archaeological and documentary evidence. Accordingly it was widely accepted and the term "New Empire" entered the nomenclature of scholars as synonymous with the era of renewed activity instituted after the abandonment of the southern regions.

But previous experience had repeatedly demonstrated the vulnerability of theorizing in the reconstruction of ancient cultures, and the problems posed by the monuments of the so-called New Empire offered no exception to this scientific axiom. Succeeding years of research made necessary an almost complete revision of their history.

When more was learned about the date inscriptions from the northern area, many of those which could be positively assigned to a place in Mayan chronology fell between the fifth and tenth centuries A.D. A door lintel from the city of Oxkintok in western Yucatán bore hieroglyphs reaching back as early as 475. At Cobá, an extensive ruin in Quintana Roo, five stelae had been erected commemorating dates between 623 and 652. A temple at Chichén Itzá bore an inscription corresponding to 879. All of these dates were parallel with the last half of the Classic period. This was a salient point indeed, for it established the fact that these cities—far distant from the supposed centers of Classic tradition—were occupied long before the abandonment of the Old Empire by groups familiar with calendrics and hieroglyphic writing as practiced in presumably older cities.

Could it still be assumed that these northern centers of activity had remained nothing more than outlying provinces during the rise of the Old Empire? Or had they actually shared in its florescence? On the basis of such contrary evidence there was reason for a much more thorough evaluation of the previous concept.

In the science of resurrecting vanished civilizations, pottery is the denominator of many things. Individual cultures and chronological sequences within those cultures are often characterized by particular types of ceramics. By means of design, materials, and execution, pottery fragments can frequently be identified as belonging to specific locales and periods of time.

Subsequent excavations in the northern Yucatán Peninsula brought to light a curious fact in this line of inquiry: a number of sites yielded types of pottery strikingly similar to that identified with Classic culture—the so-called Tzakol and Tepeuh wares. Generally, the former—the earlier of these styles—were typified by cylindrical vessels which rested on three leglike projections, and were decorated largely with geometric designs or simple figurations painted in a variety of colors. The latter or Tepeuh style represents a period of flamboyance in Mayan ceramic art—cylinders, oval jars, and bowls finely wrought and embellished with elaborate polychrome designs, including human figures and glyphs. From beneath extensive refuse heaps and the floors of buildings in northern Yucatán came many examples of superbly fashioned pottery which reflected an unmistakable affinity with these distinctive ceramic fashions so closely associated with Classic horizons.

A reappraisal of the architecture found in the northern part of the peninsula told more or less the same story as its pottery sequences. At first archaeologists had seized upon certain striking differences between structures in this area and those of the Petén and Usumacinta regions as further proof that the latter were much older and rightfully entitled to stand alone in the mainstream of the Classic tradition.

The builders of the northern cities had not arranged their structures in the strict manner usually associated with the supposedly earlier sites. Fewer terraced pyramids were to be found, and the relatively pure ornamentation of buildings had been supplanted by highly decorous façades embellished with a maze of cut stone incorporating geometric patterns of incredible complexity.

In the vicinity of the Puuc Hills—in the northwestern corner of the peninsula—this unique method of ornamentation had reached extravagant proportions. Uxmal, the foremost archaeological monument in this region, is an outstanding example of the intricacy with which these external refinements were often wrought. Yet, within a tradition of rococo-like ornateness, its builders achieved an astounding elegance and subtlety of proportion. One of its principal structures was the so-called Palace of the Governors, an elongated temple raised skyward on a broad terraced acropolis. Stephens spoke without exaggeration when he remarked of it: "There is no rudeness or barbarity in the design or proportions; on the contrary, the whole wears an air of architectural symmetry and grandeur. If it stood at this day on its grand artificial terrace in Hyde Park or the Garden

of the Tuileries, it would form a new order...not unworthy
to stand side by side with the remains of Egyptian, Grecian,
and Roman art."

But as more was learned about the evolution of Mayan
architecture, the peculiarities which distinguished Uxmal and
its neighboring cities from lowland ruins were less indicative
of a more recent origin. For instance, it had been noted that
numerous centers located immediately north of the Petén dis-
trict had developed distinctive architectural traditions at a very
early date. In areas known as the Río Bec and Chenes—roughly
in the middle of the Yucatán Peninsula—new schools of architecture had found wide expression during the centuries from
A.D. 500 to 900. Río Bec and Chenes styles were typified by the
use of heavily stuccoed masks adorning buildings, ornamental
towers incorporated into façades, and entranceways designed
in the form of open serpents' mouths. Features such as these
had not occurred in the area encompassed by Copán, Tikal, and
Palenque—the heart of the Old Empire—yet the Río Bec and
Chenes cities were unquestionably contemporary with these
centers. Why, then, was it not equally possible that the ruins
found in northern Yucatán represented still another of these
distinctive variations in architecture which flowered simultaneously with Classic culture elsewhere?

All of these factors—date inscriptions, pottery sequences,
and a closer examination of architectural styles—necessitated
broad revisions in the earlier concept of the so-called New
Empire. Far from the idea that the great centers in the northern half of the peninsula had remained nothing more than
unimportant provinces during the period from A.D. 400 to 900,
such cities as Uxmal, Labná, Cobá, and Chichén Itzá had
flourished at precisely the same time as Copán, Tikal, Yaxchilán, and Palenque. Their art, architecture, and other
cultural manifestations had been fashioned of identical components, but had matured along separate routes of expression.

Accordingly these magnificent centers had not been the crowning jewels of a "renaissance" brought about by survivors of the Old Empire. Indeed, when disaster overtook the regions to the south—when their splendid ceremonial centers were surrendered to the jungle—so, too, were the northern cities abandoned to briar thickets and fields of tangled shrubs. At Tzibanché, on the east coast of the peninsula, a jade gorget was unearthed bearing one of the latest positively known inscriptions for the northern area—A.D. 909, which approximates the closing dates established elsewhere for the Classic period. Emigrants from the south may well have found their way to northern Yucatán as the first of their cities fell to ruin. But their fortunes were no more promising: the disaster was spreading!

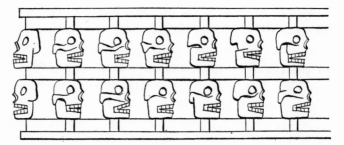

Chichén Itzá

Until this point in Mayan history—that is, until the universal abandonment of their city-states—the Maya had proceeded along a solitary course; their rise to eminence and succeeding collapse resulted from inherent factors rather than the pressure of foreign influences. Now, however, a curious new element rose out of the sea of confusion in which the Maya found themselves. Against the background of cultural stagnation, social unrest, and disillusionment which had shattered their former placidity, a radically new force seized and redirected their political and spiritual fortunes. It swept over them suddenly; in its very forcefulness Mayan civilization found a momentary renewal of its former vigor reactivated along new avenues of endeavor. It had been a virile, cogent force, but one of mysterious origin.

From where was it derived? Had it come from beyond the boundaries of the Mayan empire, most of which had fallen by then into desolate ruin? Was it wrought by wanderers from some distant place, or had it sprung from long-established traditions which had undergone angry mutations at the hands of a disillusioned populace? And what were the archaeological manifestations which hinted at the presence of these alien ideas?

Chichén Itzá—the extensive ruined city seventy miles east of Mérida in Yucatán—had long been an archaeological puzzle. It was known from the time of the Conquest, but scientists did not undertake to probe its massive structures in depth until 1924 when the Carnegie Institution began a program of excavation and reconstruction. A curious paradox emerged from its ruins: more than half of its buildings departed radically from recognized traditions of Mayan architecture. Furthermore, the design and sculptural embellishments of these spurious structures reflected non-Mayan elements which strongly hinted that alien influences had left their mark upon the city.

Etched on columns and temple walls were dozens of strangely foreign motifs—figures of warriors wearing heavy layers of cotton armor, carrying shields and spears. Everything about the dress and character of these figures was at variance with the usual concept of Mayan men of war.

Aside from these sculptural motifs, a number of new structural forms were uncovered at Chichén Itzá. One of these was a completely circular building known as the Caracol, which is believed to have been an astronomical observatory. Other structures were placed in conjunction with long rows of columns, and a large open area enclosed by colonnades suggested a possible market place. Also unique was the use of massive columns sculptured in the form of serpents which flanked the doors and stairways of temples, and the long rows of vultures holding human hearts and jaguars crouched as though ready to attack sculptured in bold relief on their walls. And lying about the city's main plaza were several monolithic figures of reclining men with raised knees and heads, holding bowl-like vessels on their abdomens—the so-called Chac Mools.

Standing in what had once been a broad plaza were the remnants of a stone platform, T-shaped in outline and faced with rows of carved human skulls. No such structure had ever before been encountered in the Mayan area, but far to the north, on the Mexican plateau, platforms such as this were known from several archaeological sites. Bernal Díaz, in his narrative of the Conquest, recorded seeing an almost identical structure in the Aztec capital city of Tenochtitlán. It was called a *tzompantli,* and contained racks on which were publicly displayed the skulls of sacrificial victims. But so far as was known, the *tzompantli* had been an exclusively Mexican innovation; its presence in northern Yucatán was noted with mounting curiosity.

Indeed, all of these non-Mayan characteristics were reminiscent of similar discoveries unearthed by archaeologists among certain ruins in the Valley of Mexico and adjacent areas. Only one explanation could satisfactorily account for their presence at Chichén Itzá: they were the indelible imprints of foreign intruders from the direction of Mexico's more warlike and sanguinary cultures who had overwhelmed the city's inhabitants and implanted among them the seeds of a radically different culture. A mural in the Temple of the Jaguars depicted lines of battle drawn between Mayan defenders and hordes of warriors whose costumes and weapons match the frozen figures uncovered so profusely on Chichén Itzá's buildings. For the first time in a graphic representation, the Maya are shown falling in defeat before their enemy!

Now, too, a strangely perplexing circumstance began to clarify itself: various native chronicles written after the Conquest mentioned the role played in the concluding centuries of Mayan history by an elusive people known as the Itzás. From the *Books of Chilam Balam* have come detailed accounts of these foreigners and of the magnificent capital they founded at Chichén Itzá following their arrival into Yucatán from Mexico. Even Bishop Landa's history includes vivid accounts of the coming of the Itzás as related by his Indian informants.

Furthermore, these historical documents describe the Itzás as having come originally from a far-distant city which was called Tollán and whose builders were known as Toltecs. They relate how the Itzás had set out from Mexico upon migratory wanderings which carried them first to Veracruz. There they split into two groups; one proceeded to the Guatemalan highlands, and the other—the larger of the two bands—made its way along the eastern coast of Mexico until it eventually arrived in Yucatán.

As they appeared at a time coincident with the outbreak of turmoil among the Maya, their entry presented much less of a military obstacle than they might have otherwise encountered. Ensnared in their own internal difficulties, the Maya had been virtually helpless to offer sustained resistance to the persuasive will of the Itzás and had submitted to the imposition of new laws and religious manifestations. By the beginning of the eleventh century the intruders were in firm control of the former seats of power.

But what of the evasive city of Tollán and its little-known inhabitants, the Toltecs? And what archaeological evidence was there to indicate that these legends might have been rooted in historical fact?

Myths concerning ancient Tollán were far from unique when they were first encountered in Yucatán. Archaeologists had long pondered over various similar accounts inherited from sixteenth-century historians, but to little avail in estab-

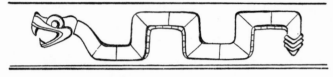

Chichén Itzá

lishing their authenticity. A Franciscan friar, Bernardino de Sahagún, was perhaps the first chronicler to mention Tollán in his monumental journal entitled *A General History of the Things of New Spain.* For some sixty years after the conquest of Mexico Sahagún had labored at transcribing the language, customs, and mythology of the Aztecs into a bilingual record, utilizing their native Nahuatl dialect and Spanish. With much the same determination as Bishop Landa had pursued his studies of the Yucatecans, Sahagún worked among the Aztecs, questioning them about every detail of their history and beliefs. One fact was persistently confirmed by his informants: their major cultural accruements—art and architecture, the calendar, and the essential tenets of their religion—had been handed down to them by a people who had inhabited the Valley of Mexico centuries before the Aztecs established their reign early in the fourteenth century. According to the information gleaned by Sahagún, these earlier tribesmen were actually the mysterious Toltecs, and the center of their authority was a magnificent city known as Tollán.

In his voluminous chronicle, Friar Sahagún related that the Toltecs "were highly skilled. Nothing that they did was difficult for them. . . . They cut green stone [jade], and they cast gold,

and they made other works of the craftsman and the feather-
worker. Very skilled were they ...

"And these Toltecs enjoyed great wealth; they were rich;
never were they poor. Nothing did they lack in their homes. . . .
And the small ears of maize were of no use to them; they only
[burned them to] heat their sweat baths." *

A sixteenth-century Aztec noble, one Fernando de Alva
Ixtlilxochitl—an interpreter for the Spanish viceroy—had also
devoted a prodigious amount of effort to writing a lengthy
account of his people's history. His version strongly corroborated the facts as recorded by Sahagún: the great civilizing
force underlying the rise of high cultures in the Valley of
Mexico was originally derived from Toltec inspiration. He
portrayed them as masters of art, medicine, calendrics, and
engineering; they were fiercely religious and given to rich
pageantry. Toltec rule was strict but justly enforced, and their
cherished leader was known as Quetzalcoatl, the mighty
Plumed Serpent—the "living divinity who dwelled among the
builders of Tollán." But inherent seeds of decay had finally
disrupted their prosperity. Drought, pestilence, and famine
brought on civil strife, and prompted hostile tribes to attack
the weakened Toltecs. Eventually they had been forced to
abandon Tollán and venture south in search of a new domain.
Thus, according to legend, had they found their way to
Yucatán.

In weighing the evidence for and against the validity of
these accounts, archaeologists were confronted with certain
obvious facts. All of the post-Conquest narratives agreed without qualification that Aztec culture had drawn its initial in-

* Anderson, Arthur J. O., and Charles E. Dibble (translators and editors):
Florentine Codex: General History of the Things of New Spain, by Fray
Bernardino de Sahagún. Book III, *The Origin of the Gods* (Santa Fe: School of
American Research, Monograph No. 14, Part 4, and University of Utah, 1952),
pp. 13-14.

spiration, at least in part, from the Toltecs who preceded them, and that the ancestral home of these civilizers had been the place called Tollán.

Furthermore, scattered throughout the Valley of Mexico and its surrounding environs were ruins of obviously greater antiquity than those of Aztec origin. Foremost among these was the ceremonial city of San Juan de Teotihuacán, thirty miles north of Mexico City. Its massive pyramids of the Sun and Moon, its lavish temple dedicated to the elusive Quetzalcoatl, and the dozens of smaller structures arranged along grand processional avenues had made it a center of first importance in ancient times. But Teotihuacán was already in ruins when the Aztecs founded their capital on the present site of Mexico City in A.D. 1325. Elsewhere in the vicinity were still other crumbled reminders of former grandeurs. Obviously the Aztecs had arrived on the scene only in time to reclaim something of the intellectual precocity still retained by their survivors; that much was amply confirmed by archeological findings.

For lack of a more definitive term this cultural substratum won for itself the designation "Toltec," and virtually all the archaeological remains in and around the Valley of Mexico were attributed to the so-called "Toltec" culture. Recent excavations have ruled out the literal implications of this once widely accepted concept. It has been positively demonstrated that the Toltecs did not occupy the cultural stage in the Valley of Mexico exclusively: other groups were equally responsible for its archaeological splendors. Even Teotihuacán had apparently lived out the significant years of his history some years before the Toltecs rose to prominence.

However, there could be no doubt, even from a surface examination, that certain distinctive features evidenced by ruins in and adjacent to the Valley of Mexico were strongly reminiscent of those which distinguished Chichén Itzá from ordinary

The Temple of the Sun, Palenque.

Detail of a sculptured balustrade in the east court of the Great Plaza, Palenque.

A portion of the stucco relief adorning the pilasters of the Great Palace, Palenque.

The Great Palace, Palenque.

Interior of the burial vault at Palenque showing the sculptured slab in its original position. (*Courtesy Instituto Nacional de Antropologia e Historia, Mexico*)

The sarcophagus containing the remains of the high priest surrounded by jade ornaments, Palenque. (*Courtesy Instituto Nacional de Antropologia e Historia, Mexico*)

Stucco sculpture from the burial vault, the Temple of the Inscriptions, Palenque. (*National Museum of Mexico*)

A Lacandon man from Lake Lacanja, Chiapas. (*Courtesy Giles Healey*)

Jade mosaic death mask found in the grave of a high priest, Temple of the Inscriptions, Palenque. (*National Museum of Mexico*)

Details of murals, Bonampak. Above, five *batabs* or priests in ceremonial costume. Below, a procession of musicians. (*From reproductions in the National Museum of Mexico by Augustin Villagra Caleti.*)

A Lacandon burning *copal* at the ruins of Yaxchilan, Chiapas. He holds a board containing nodules of the sacred incense. (*Courtesy Giles Healey*)

A *caribal* near Lake Miramar, Chiapas. (*Courtesy Giles Healey*)

The Great Palace, Labna.

The Palace, Sayil.

The Palace of the Governors, Uxmal.

Interior view, Palace of the Governors, Uxmal.

Facade of the west wing, The Nunnery Quadrangle, Uxmal.

The Temple of Kukulcan, Chichén Itzá.

A view of three principal structures at Chichén Itzá: foreground, The Observatory; in the background, The Temple of Kukulcan and The Temple of the Warriors.

The Temple of the Warriors, Chichén Itzá.

The Well of Sacrifice, Chichén Itzá.

The Observatory viewed from a temple known as La Iglesia, Chichén Itzá.

Portion of a mural depicting a battle, Temple of the Jaguars, Chichén Itzá.

Detail of a column showing an "Itza" warrior, The Temple of the Warriors, Chichén Itzá.

Mayan cities. But the problem remained to locate positively the legendary Tollán—the place from which Toltec civilization had supposedly emanated in the Valley of Mexico—if, indeed, the long-missing city had ever existed at all. Many scholars of eminent reputation denounced the serious pursuit of such fantasies; they even refused to sanction the rhetorical use of the word Toltec, claiming that without absolute proof that such a culture had once flourished its application was misleading. Others, however, were not so willing to disregard the value of legend in reconstructing historical occurrences.

Roughly fifty-four miles northwest of Mexico City, in the state of Hidalgo, a small town known as Tula nestles in a sun-parched valley. On a limestone promontory overlooking the dusty village, several dozen rubble-covered mounds were all that remained of what had once been a flourishing settlement. Fernando de Alva Ixtlilxochitl had claimed Tula as the actual site of vanished Tollán. In 1880 the noted French traveler and antiquarian, Désiré Charnay, remarked with more than passing interest that certain monuments which he uncovered at Tula were duplicated at Chichén Itzá, but the ruins long eluded the serious inquiry of archaeologists. Like the numerous other archaeological sites in the Valley of Mexico, it was regarded as a site of secondary importance to the more impressive Teotihuacán. However, in 1940, a group of Mexican researchers began to explore Tula systematically; shovels broke through the hard crust of earth which sealed the underlying ruins from view. Beneath the rubble of untold centuries lay yet another startling discovery. Charnay's observations had indeed been accurate!

Out of these excavations there gradually emerged the entire panorama of traits so clearly identified with Chichén Itzá. Where formerly the similarities between that great Mayan metropolis and ruins in central Mexico were suggested only by subtle likenesses, at Tula they were resoundingly confirmed.

Here were the same figures of armored warriors which adorned
Chichén Itzá, the knights who had carried the bitter taste of
conquest to the Maya. Identical frescoes of jaguars and vultures feeding upon human hearts moved across the walls of
Tula's pyramids, and there were long rows of inscribed square
columns which could easily have been interchanged with those
found at the Mayan City. A reclining figure of a Chac Mool,
alike in every detail to the several unearthed near the *tzompantli* in Chichén Itzá's main plaza, was found at the base of a
pyramid at Tula. So, too, were curious sculptures of dwarfs
with upraised hands—"Atlantean" figures as they were mis-
named by Augustus Le Plongeon, who had discovered identical
forms in the ruins of Chichén Itzá eighty years earlier. Tula
had once boasted of several ball courts, massive caryatids representing ceremonially attired warriors, sunken plazas, walls of
carved serpents, and beautifully designed altars, many of which
were decorated with skull motifs. And everywhere were images
of the adored priest-god Quetzalcoatl—rattlesnakes bedecked
with plumes. So striking were the similarities between Tula
and Chichén Itzá that it seemed as though the same artists
and engineers had worked first at one location and then at
the other. Eight hundred land miles of difficult and, in the
prehistoric past, hostile terrain separated the two sites, yet
their cultural affinity was undeniable.

A degree of credibility could also be afforded the accounts
of Tula's final downfall. Excavations determined that sometime around A.D. 1168 invading armies, preying upon internal
weaknesses and civil strife then rampant among the Toltecs,
brought about its destruction. Its inhabitants were banished
from the area and forced to settle elsewhere. Long before
that, however, waves of Toltec peoples had begun a series of
southward migrations, lured perhaps by rumored splendors
of the distant Mayan empire. And there can be little question
on the basis of the archaeological evidence already cited that

the so-called "Itzás" were in reality Toltec emigrants derived from Tula—the long-missing city of Tollán.

But they did not come as tattered refugees of previous misfortunes. Their once-powerful armies were reassembled and revived by the spirit of new conquests. Behind the proud legions of knights were streams of colonists bent upon restoring their former prosperity. Discipline among them was strict, and they possessed a confidence rooted in an ancient tradition of militarism. Like most of the peoples of the Mexican plateau, these Toltec tribesmen had not shared the Mayan ideals of temperance and moderation: they were warriors in the service of their more bloodthirsty gods.

And so the Toltecs—whom the Maya called the Itzás— moved into the Yucatán Peninsula. Here and there the Maya perhaps rallied from the strife which had brought their history to a standstill, drawing lines of battle against the intruders. Pounding drums and the shriek of conch-shell trumpets were soon drowned in the shouts of men hurled together in furious conflict. Mayan blood was spilled in defeat and the victorious Itzás marched on past cities which were splendid beyond comparison—and desolate.

A few were still sparsely occupied: Uxmal, perhaps Kabah, and Chichén Itzá, then known by another name. But this latter city was more populous than the others; its inhabitants had not retreated to villages of stucco and thatched huts, leaving the ceremonial structures to decay and crumble. Under the guardianship of still-powerful priests the temples had retained their opulent splendor. It was a sprawling metropolis laid out upon a broad plain surrounded by prosperous milpas and a series of natural wells. Here, decreed the Itzás, they would found a new capital.

In essence, then, most of what the *Books of Chilam Balam* and Bishop Landa's account had related concerning the coming of the Itzás had been borne out by archaeological research, though certain vital details of these occurrences are still obscure. How long did the Toltec migrations from Mexico continue? Were the Itzás of pure Toltec extraction, or a mixture of peoples allied with them during their gradual exodus to the south? And towering above all of these enigmas was the legend of the powerful Toltec leader Quetzalcoatl—the man-god known to the Maya as Kukulcan.

Uxmal

Numerous conflicting myths describe the epochal accomplishments of Quetzalcoatl. Supposedly he had been a lord of Tollán whose munificence and wisdom won for his memory a place of supreme eminence in the Toltec pantheon. "Quetzalcoatl they say was he who created the world; and they bestowed upon him the appellation of Lord of the Wind, because they said that Tonacatecotli [a creator-god, the father of Quetzalcoatl] . . . breathed and begat Quetzalcoatl. They erected round temples to him. . . . They said that it was he who formed the first man. . . . He alone had a human body like that of men; the other gods were of an incorporeal nature."

Eventually Quetzalcoatl was betrayed by jealous warrior gods and driven from the Valley of Mexico. Some said that he vanished into the sea near Veracruz, others proclaimed that he eventually ascended into the heavens and became the morning star. Yet another account related that the man "whom they called Quetzalcoatl . . . taught them [his followers] by word and deed the way of virtue, saving them from vice and sin, giving them laws and good doctrine; and to restrain them in their lusts and lewd ways, had instituted fasting amongst them. . . . But seeing how little fruit his doctrine brought forth, he had gone away by the same road he had come, which was to the East, vanishing on the Coast of Coatzacoalco, and as he parted from them, he had said to them that at a future time ... he would return, and then his doctrine would be received, and his sons would be lords and owners of the lands, which they and their descendants would undergo many calamities and persecutions. ..."

Quetzalcoatl's veneration spread far beyond the geographical and chronological limits of Toltec influence. He was known throughout Mexico; his emblem—a feathered serpent—is found everywhere in Mexican antiquity. Montezuma—the emperor of the Aztec nation—yielded before Hernan Cortéz in the belief that he was actually the cherished Quetzalcoatl returning from the dead—so vivid was his image and the words of his prophecy a thousand years after his departure.

Native sources relate that it had been Quetzalcoatl himself who actually led the Itzás in their conquest of Yucatán. To the Maya he was known as Kukulcan, and his veneration became as profound as it was among the Mexicans. Bishop Landa wrote of him: "It is believed among the Indians that with the Itzás who occupied Chichén Itzá there reigned a great lord, named Kukulcan, and that the principal building, which is called Kukulcan, shows this to be true [a reference to El Castillo or the Temple of Kukulcan]. They say that he arrived from the west; but they differ among themselves as to whether he arrived before or after the Itzás or with them. They say that he was favorably disposed, and had no wife or children, and that after his return he was regarded in Mexico as one of their gods and called Quetzalcoatl; and they also considered him a god in Yucatán on account of his being a just statesman; and this is seen in the order which he imposed on Yucatán after the death of the lords [the overthrow of Mayan rule by the Itzás], in order to calm the dissensions which their deaths had caused in the country."

But had there been actually such a man as Quetzalcoatl—one whose precocity was perhaps amplified by succeeding generations until his memory was deified? Archaeologists agree there might well have been a ruler of his supposed abilities at Tollán. It has also been suggested that he may have founded a dynasty of successors who bore his name. Quetzalcoatl is generally described as having been a bearded man with fair skin, and during his rule it was said that he journeyed about the countryside instilling tolerance and justice among his adoring subjects. Yet according to other sources his fame rested on the very antithesis of such beliefs: he was renowned for his military prowess and territorial conquests. It is curious that Landa's informants described this same hero—Kukulcan—as a temperate and just statesman while archaeology has confirmed the warlike qualities of his Itzá followers who brought a new way of life to Yucatán.

Very likely this alien colonization occurred gradually, bringing with it profound alterations in the old order of things. Art, architecture, and social traditions underwent severe aberrations away from long-established Mayan norms toward the more persuasive Toltec point of view. Religious practices, especially, were radically altered by the introduction of Toltec gods whose character differed in many respects from those so long venerated by the Maya. George Brainerd stated in the revision of Morley's *The Ancient Maya* that "respect for the piety of Kukulcan and the luxuriance of religious construction at Chichén Itzá suggest that the Maya may have lent their talents and labors willingly to the furtherance of a new religion. Perhaps the Toltec conquest of Yucatán was accomplished as much by religious evangelization as by military force." *

However it was brought about, Itzá-Toltec rule was firmly

* Reprinted from *The Ancient Maya,* by Sylvanus G. Morley, with the permission of the publishers, Stanford University Press. Copyright 1946, 1947, and 1956 by the Board of Trustees of Leland Stanford Junior University.

imposed on Yucatán by A.D. 1000. Eventually Toltec influence made its way into every facet of Mayan culture, and Chichén Itzá became the center from which Itzá political domination was to spread in many directions throughout the Yucatán Peninsula. Yet it is abundantly clear that Mayan civilization did not wither away under Itzá subjugation, nor did it suffer annihilation by military force. In time, intermarriage and cultural exchange presaged the fusion of native and foreign traditions into a compatible mixture of traits.

But the great Classic tradition was forever dead; never again would the Maya be able to regain the heights they had once known. Even the vigor imparted to them by the Itzás, the overwhelming stimulation of the fierce Mexican gods, and the pomp of grand armies that marched in their behalf, the zeal with which Mayan craftsmen labored to remodel Chichén Itzá in the image of their new overlords, could not long forestall the disaster that awaited them.

ARCHAEOLOGICAL DIVISIONS OF MAYAN HISTORY

B.C. 2000 to 500	Archaic	A.D. 925 to 1200	Post-Classic New Empire
500 to A.D. 325	Formative	1200 to 1540	Mexican Absorption
325 to 925	Classic Old Empire	1540	Post-Conquest

One of the singularly outstanding monuments of the new order implanted at Chichén Itzá was the so-called Temple of the Warriors. When the great mound under which it was concealed was first laid bare in 1925 by the Carnegie Institution, its size and volume of debris were all that remained to suggest that a splendid edifice had once stood on the site opposite the lofty Temple of Kukulcan in the city's northern plaza. At the base of its barely distinguishable remains were fragments of dozens of square columns which had once formed an impressive colonnade along the front of the terraced building, and almost all the columns bore the weathered image of Itzá warriors.

Under the skilled supervision of Earl H. Morris, who was placed in charge of the project, a crew of native laborers began the arduous task of excavating and restoring the fallen temple as near its original splendor as possible. More telltale imprints of Itzá workmanship were unearthed as the work progressed: a broken Chac Mool, a number of Atlantean figures, and sections of huge columns sculptured in the form of plumed serpents which had originally been set up on either side of the temple's doorway.

After several full seasons of excavation, the pristine elegance of the Temple of the Warriors began to emerge from the rubble; it had long before merited pronouncement as an architectural masterpiece. Its lines were angular, its design dramatically executed and spoke well of its Toltec inspiration. Large sections of its white limestone walls were embellished by panels of sculptured masks, serpents, vultures, and jaguars in perfect proportion with the building's other decorative elements.

Within the core of the structure an inner chamber was found which contained murals and four painted warrior columns in a remarkable state of preservation. But this "buried temple" retained an even more startling legacy of its builders. Morris had explored several altars uncovered in various portions of the building in the hope of finding offertory objects placed beneath them by priests. His search had been unrewarding. Ultimately he decided to probe a section of the buried

temple where another such altar had once rested. Preliminary
soundings revealed a hollow area underneath the floor; quickly
he picked open a small opening directly above it. "I thrust my
fingers into the hole . . ." he wrote, "and raised a lid of stone.
From the bottom of the cylindrical recess which it had shielded
there came the gleam of polished jade. . . ."

Later the same afternoon, Morris returned to the scene
of his discovery accompanied by Sylvanus Morley and other
visiting dignitaries of the Carnegie Institution. "At the center
of the circular cavity," he related, "lay a ball of jade that had
reached well above the thin film of lime powder that had
worked into the container during the long interval of its inter-
ment. Beside the ball, partly obscured by the white film, was an
irregular shaped plaque of jade, the surface toward us graven
to represent a human face. At either end of it was a small
sphere of jade, and scattered about in disorder were many
beads of shell. That much was visible at first glance. With a
long handled camel's-hair brush . . . I began to sweep toward
one edge of the cavity the powdered lime that partially hid
the beads. The fourth or fifth stroke of the brush left behind
it a trail of robin's-egg blue such as I expect never again to
behold. In sheer astonishment I held the brush poised an
instant, fortunately as it happened, for there came a mighty
whack on my shoulder from Doctor Morley's hand, as he
shouted,

" 'Old man, it's a turquoise mosaic. Hurry up and see how
big it is.' "

Lying in the stone jar was a superbly wrought plaque, meas-
uring some nine inches in diameter and composed of almost
three thousand individual pieces of polished turquoise. "We
had come upon an archeological treasure of unparalleled
rarity," concluded Morris, ". . . the plaque was the most exquisite example of aboriginal American craftsmanship that
any of us had ever seen come from the earth."

CHAPTER 12

The Well of Sacrifice

EDWARD HERBERT THOMPSON was barely twenty-five years of age when he was appointed to the post of United States consul to Yucatán in 1885. Like Stephens, his illustrious predecessor, the responsibilities of a diplomatic career were of secondary importance to his passion for archaeology. From his early youth Thompson had been an avid student of Mayan antiquities, and the focal point of his interest was to become the acres of partly collapsed structures and littered mounds that had once been the lofty city of Chichén Itzá.

Some years after his arrival on the scene Thompson negotiated for the purchase of the hacienda on which the ruins were located. At that point practically nothing was known of Chichén Itzá's history. It had been explored by various travelers—among them Waldeck, Stephens, Le Plongeon, Charnay, and Maudslay—all of whom belonged to the nineteenth century in which occurred the erratic birth of Mayan archaeology out of a labyrinth of bewildering enigmas. Thompson had no more insight into the multiple complexities of Mayan lore than those before him; he had, in fact, once championed lost Atlantis as the birthplace of Mayan culture. But he possessed imagination, and, more important, the determination to test the validity of his convictions.

In the account of his numerous adventures entitled *People of the Serpent,* Thompson described his first impression of the ruined city that was to be his home for thirty years:

The gradual ascent and winding of the trail between the boulders and the big trees seemed so like familiar forest rambles at home that it came over me almost with a shock to realize that the boulders I passed by so carelessly had cut surfaces and were once carved columns and sculptured pillars. Then, just as I began to understand that the level, forest-covered surface beneath my feet was a terrace made by ancient man, I peered upward to a great stone mass that pierced the sky, and all else was forgotten. A pyramid with terraced sides, paneled walls of cut limestone, and broad stairways leading upward was crowned by a temple. Other buildings, high mounds, and broken terraces were buried in the forest and only the dark green knobs on the horizon told where they stood.

Pen cannot describe or brush portray the strange feelings produced by the beating of the tropic sun against the ash-colored walls of those venerable structures. Old . . . furrowed by time, and haggard, imposing, and impassive, they rear their rugged masses above the surrounding level and are beyond description.

The ruined group of Chichén Itzá covers a space of fully three square miles. Over all this territory are scattered carved and square stones in countless thousands and fallen columns by the hundreds; while the formless remains and outlined walls of huge structures fallen into decay are seen on every side. Seven massive structures of carved stone and adamantine mortar still tower erect and almost habitable. Their façades, though gray and haggard with age and seamed by time, sustain the claim that Chichén Itzá is one of the world's greatest monuments to antiquity.

Near the center of the city's main plaza there stood a massive pyramid known today as El Castillo or the Temple of Kukulcan. It rose in a series of diminishing terraces to tower some seventy-five feet above the surrounding plain. It measured sixty yards along each base, and four wide stairways ascended to a superb temple at the summit. The structure's design is essentially of Toltec inspiration, but Mayan rules of astronomical orientation were applied to its construction. Each of the four stairways had ninety-one steps; the addition of an upper platform made a total of three hundred and sixty-five—the number of days in the civil year. Its nine terraces were divided into fifty-two panels, which is equivalent to the number of years in the ceremonial cycle of the Toltec calendar; and these terraces, in turn, were separated by the stairways into eighteen sections, or the number of months in the Mayan year. Excavations have since revealed the presence of an inner pyramid within the present structure, and an antechamber therein contained a sculptured figure of the Chac Mool type with mother-of-pearl inlaid in the eyes, teeth, and fingernails, together with a magnificently carved jaguar throne.

During the years Thompson resided at Chichén Itzá, he examined nearly all of its structures and encountered numerous discoveries of importance. Several hundred yards south of the Temple of Kukulcan stood the remains of a low pyramid. Nothing about the formless mound of rubble was especially conspicuous except its four stairways which were flanked by stone balustrades in the form of open-jawed serpents. Its summit, in characteristic fashion, had once been crowned by a temple; four elaborately carved columns were all that remained of the ceremonial structure. It was while excavating portions of the best preserved of these columns that Thompson stumbled upon two highly polished cap stones imbedded in what had once been the floor of the temple.

On a vague hunch he raised the stones and found below them the outline of a square shaft descending approximately twelve feet into the pyramid. Faintly discernible on the floor of the vault was a human skeleton surrounded by earthen vessels. The remains were resting on another smooth flagstone similar to those which had sealed the upper entrance. Below this were four more graves superimposed upon one another. "In the third grave," Thompson wrote, "I found a handful of copper bells, small in size, and turned to verdigris. In the fourth I found a necklace of handsomely cut and finely polished rock-crystal beads. The floor of this last grave was on a level with the base of the pyramid, and I naturally concluded that, as the pyramid rested on the limestone ledge rock of the region, my work of excavation was automatically ended. Then I observed that the stone floor tiles still persisted and, lifting them, I discovered to my surprise a series of steps hewn out of the living rock down into a chamber. . . . The stairs were covered and the chamber filled with wood ashes. The only way I could enter . . . was by lying flat on my back and pushing my feet ahead of me through the ashes and into the chamber. . . ."

Slowly Thompson worked his way into the ash-filled crypt. Intermingled with the refuse which he began clearing from the floor were quantities of jade beads, some of which looked as though they had been burned. The vault was empty except for a square stone slab resting against one wall.

He grasped it with both hands and began to pull. Unexpectedly it gave way, revealing a black hole in the floor below. A flood of cold air rushed out of the cavernous opening, blowing out candles and leaving Thompson and his assistants in "utter darkness in the bowels of the earth."

"Don Eduardo," cried his natives, "this is surely the mouth of Hell!"

"Not so," he replied. "Since when has the mouth of Hell given forth a breath as cold as this wind?"

By a curious irony this logic appealed to the terrified Indians. Christian teachings had instilled in them the European concept of Hell as a blazing inferno where the condemned suffered fiery ordeals. Had they still adhered to the beliefs of their ancestors—that *Mitnal,* or Hell, was a place of unbearable cold—they would surely have fled amid shrieks of terror as the cold air issued from the ominous black pit.

The opening was roughly circular in outline and three feet in diameter. By lowering a lantern attached to a rope, Thompson estimated its depth to be fifty feet. "I had two of the natives grasp each of my feet at the ankle, and then, head downward, my body swinging like a pendulum with my tape and light below me, I managed to get a good idea of the place. . . .

"After getting back my breath, I told my workers that we would . . . return very early on the morrow prepared to go down into that hole. I also warned them not to tell anybody what we were doing lest they laugh at us and call us crazy. As a matter of fact, I was certain that we had made a very important find, and I did not want any more witnesses than I could help."

By dawn Thompson's native crew had assembled at the pyramid for the day's adventure. A block and tackle was mounted above the opening in order to haul up the debris from the pit. Equipped with a knife between his teeth, his pockets bulging with trowels, brushes, candles, and an odd assortment of other materials, Thompson was lowered by a rope through the shaft and into the cold black pit beneath its floor.

Scarcely had he switched on his lantern when there lay before him an unexpected treasure—a superbly fashioned vase of translucent alabaster. It was filled with polished jade beads and a single jade pendant. A few moments later his assistants, eager with expectation, had scrambled down the rope and were beside him.

During the hours that followed they were lost in the feverish excitement of discovery. One after another, magnificent relics were exhumed from the debris on the floor of the cavern. Scattered about were large shells inlaid with mother-of-pearl, painted earthenware jars and bowls, ceremonial flint blades resembling "the votive stone sickles of the ancient Druids," and numbers of large oval pearls, many of which had laid so long undisturbed that they fell to powder at the slightest touch.

We ate and drank as the spirit moved us and then continued with the work until I could feel that a weariness was creeping over us. I gave the signal to stop work and get ready to go up into the outer world. When we reached the temple platform with our trophies, we saw a strange sight.

It was eleven o'clock in the evening. . . . A darkness as of midnight was all about us and on the plains beneath the families of my workmen were crying and lamenting, with my wife and children trying in vain to calm them.

"No use!" they wailed. "The master and all of our people are dead and gone. The Great Serpent has taken them and we shall never see them again."

Great was the rejoicing when we triumphantly appeared with our trophies and came down to them.

This was a red-letter day in my life as an archaeologist. I had discovered and investigated what was probably the sepulcher of a high priest. . . .

The five graves in the vertical shaft above . . . what of them? Whose bones, decayed and turning to dust, rested in the graves when I first uncovered them? Were they the acolytes or the servants of the high priests whose bodies were so placed as to guard in death as they had served in life this high and sacred personage? Or were they priests of a lower order, whose friends sought for them by this last close contact a higher place in the future life? Who knows?

But a discovery of far greater magnitude awaited Thompson's restless curiosity. In the midst of his speculations he was seized by an obsession that was to endanger his life, subject him to ridicule, and ultimately revoke his diplomatic license. It was also to place him among the foremost contributors to archaeological research.

Leading from one side of the Temple of Kukulcan was the outline of a road which extended some three hundred yards through the main plaza to the jungle-rimmed mouth of a cavernous well. Formations of this kind—known as *cenotes*—are common in the northern portion of the Yucatán Peninsula. They are deep natural depressions in the limestone surface and are fed by subterranean streams. As there are no rivers or lakes anywhere in the area, *cenotes* provide the only source of water, and wherever they are found ruins are certain to be close at hand.

Chichén Itzá derived its name from three large *cenotes* on the outskirts of the city. Literally the word *chi* is translated as mouth, *chen* signifies a well. Thus the words Chichén Itzá are interpreted as "The Mouth of the Well of the Itzá." One of these *cenotes* in particular aroused Thompson's curiosity. It was roughly two hundred feet in diameter and encased by vertical limestone walls that rose to a height of sixty feet from the surface of its murky green waters. At the well's mouth stood the remains of a small temple. This was the place to which legends and native chroniclers had referred: the Sacred Cenote, the Well of Sacrifice whose black depths were rumored to contain a treasure.

Bishop Landa himself had stood at the brink of the evil-looking pool and recalled its awesome secret as it was fixed in the memory of his scribes. "According to these traditions," wrote Thompson, ". . . in times of drought, pestilence, or disaster, solemn processions of priests, devotees with rich offerings, and victims for the sacrifice wound down the steep stairway of the Temple of Kukulcan, the Sacred Serpent, and along the Sacred Way to the Well of Sacrifice. There, amid the droning boom of the *tunkul,* the shrill pipings of the whistle and the plaintive notes of the flute, beautiful maidens and captive warriors of renown, as well as rich treasures, were thrown into the dark waters of the Sacred Well to propitiate the angry gods who, it was believed, lived in the deeps of the pool."

Vivid legends among the living inhabitants of Yucatán supported this belief. Often, it was said, their ancestors had fed hungering gods—especially Yum Chac, the Water Spirit— upon the flesh of living sacrifices cast into the slimy well. The Sacred Cenote was still a place of superstitious terror. To most scholars such accounts were nothing more than fantasies unworthy of further consideration. Thompson did not share their skepticism. ". . . The thought of that grim old water pit," he wrote, "and the wonderful objects that lay concealed within its depths became an obsession with me. . . ."

Then Thompson came across yet another account written by one Diego Sarmiento de Figueroa, the alcalde of Madrid who had visited Yucatán in the sixteenth century, which confirmed Landa's description:

"The lords and principal personages of the land had the custom, after sixty days of abstinence and fasting, of arriving by daybreak at the mouth of the Cenote and throwing into it Indian women belonging to each of these lords and personages, at the same time telling these women to ask for their masters a year favorable to his particular needs and desires.

"The women, being thrown in unbound, fell into the water with great force and noise. At high noon those that could cried out loudly and ropes were let down to them. After the women came up, half dead, fires were built around them and copal incense was burned before them. When they recovered their senses, they said that below there were many people of their nation, men and women, and that they received them. When they tried to raise their heads to look at them, heavy blows were given them on the head, and when their heads were inclined downward beneath the water they seemed to see many deeps and hollows, and they, the people, responded to their queries concerning the good or the bad year that was in store for their masters."

"For days and weeks after I purchased the plantation," wrote Thompson, "I was a frequent worshiper at the little shrine on the brink of the Sacred Well. I pondered, mused, and calculated. I made measurements and numberless soundings. . . ." A daring plan was taking shape in Thompson's mind. If he was to establish the validity of the myth which had so captured his imagination it would be necessary to probe beneath the well's surface for relics of the gruesome homage supposedly paid by the ancient Maya to their gods.

Before proceeding with his formidable undertaking, Thompson journeyed to Boston where he sought instruction in deep-sea diving and familiarized himself with all manner of underwater equipment. Next he designed and assembled a portable derrick and dredging apparatus suitable to his specialized needs, a device that could be mounted on a platform at the well's edge and operated by a winch.

"Then, and not until then," he wrote, "did I appear before the Honorable Stephen Salisbury of Worcester, Massachusetts, and Charles P. Bowditch of Boston, both officers of the American Antiquarian Society and of Harvard University of which the Peabody Museum is a part. To them I explained the project and asked the moral and financial aid of the two organizations they represented. . . . I found both of these gentlemen very reluctant to put the seal of their approval upon what they clearly believed to be a most audacious undertaking. They were willing to finance the scheme, but hesitated to take upon themselves the responsibility for my life.

"I finally argued them out of their fears, and all other obstacles having been overcome, the dredge and its equipment were duly installed on the platform to the right of the shrine and close to the edge of the great water pit, the Sacred Well."

Thus began a significant chapter in the history of exploration: underwater archaeology—now an exacting science as evidenced by the startling discoveries of Jacques-Yves Cousteau, Fernand Benoit, and others—was first applied to Mayan research at the mouth of Chichén Itzá's mysterious *cenote*.

With a group of Indian assistants to manage the heavy equipment, the dredging operation was finally begun. Thompson had previously determined the areas of the pool most likely to contain human remains by throwing logs the size and weight of an average man into the well from the raised temple. Slowly the rigid boom swung into position over the designated spot, and the dredge was lowered toward the water.

At last the long-planned quest was launched. Lurking in Thompson's thoughts was the avowed skepticism of his fellow antiquarians; at the outset it appeared their pronouncements were justified. For days the dredging continued with monotonous repetition; the heavy steel bucket disappeared into the well's unknown depths only to reappear with nothing but mud and decayed wood in its jaws.

"At times," recalled Thompson, "as if to tantalize me, the dredge recovered portions of earthen vessels undeniably ancient. I resolutely threw aside the thought that these might be the proofs I sought. Potsherds, I argued, were likely to be found anywhere on the site of this old city, washed from the surface deposits by rain. I could not accept these . . . as the proofs that I required."

Not long thereafter something was revealed that rekindled Thompson's fading expectations. "I remember it as if it were but yesterday," he wrote. "I rose in the morning from a sleepless night. The day was gray as my thoughts and the thick mist dropped from the leaves of the trees as quiet tears from half-closed eyes. I plodded through the dampness down to where the staccato clicks of the dredge brake called me and, crouching under the palm leaf lean-to, watched the monotonous motions of the brown-skinned natives as they worked at the winches. The bucket slowly emerged from the heaving water that boiled around it and . . . I saw two yellow-white, globular masses lying on the surface of the chocolate-colored muck that filled the basin. As the mass swung over the brink and up to the platform, I took from it the two objects and closely examined them."

Obviously they had been fashioned by human hands, but Thompson was uncertain as to what their purpose might have been. He broke one in half and tasted it; then it occurred to him to hold the substance over lighted embers. Instantly a pungent fragrance filled the air, and there flashed through Thompson's memory a detail of an age-old legend he had heard long before. "Like a ray of sunlight breaking through a dense fog came to me the words of the old *H'Men,* the Wise Man of Ebtun: 'In ancient times our fathers burned the sacred resin... and by the fragrant smoke their prayers were wafted to their God whose home was in the sun.'

"These yellow balls of resin were masses of the sacred incense *pom* [*copal*], and had been thrown in as part of the rich offerings mentioned in the traditions."

Thereafter each dredge load of the slimy mud contained new affirmation of his conviction. Out of the pit's mysterious depths came a profuse array of objects bearing the unmistakable imprint of Mayan craftsmanship: "a great store of symbolical figures carved on jade stone and beaten on gold and copper disks, copal masses, and nodules of resin incense ...a number of *hul ches,* or dart throwers, and many darts with finely worked points of flint, calcite, and obsidian...." Only during the concluding centuries of their history had the peoples of Middle America discovered the smelting of metals, and the Maya-Toltec inhabitants of Chichén Itzá had lavished what must then have been extravagant quantities of decorative metal upon the pleasure of their gods. Thompson extricated dozens of tiny bells, figurines, pendants, axeheads, and disks fashioned of copper and gold. "Objects of nearly pure gold," he wrote, "were encountered, both cast, beaten, and engraved in repousse, but they were few in number and relatively unimportant. Most of the so-called gold objects were of low-grade alloy, with more copper than gold in them. That which gave them their chief value were the symbolical and other figures cast or carved on them." At last came the ultimate measure of proof which Thompson had hoped to recover: numbers of human skeletons were brought up amid the other treasures so long immersed in Yum Chac's water shrine!

After many months the dredging operations reached an impasse: the basin began to emerge with nothing but silt and sticks caught up in its steel jaws. Obviously it had eaten its way to the floor of the pool. Thompson had anticipated such an eventuality; he planned now to descend into the well and explore its hidden crevices which the dredge was too large to reach. The necessary equipment was already at his disposal, and he had previously engaged two Greek sponge divers to assist with his precarious explorations. To the horror of the Indians who crowded around the rim of the *cenote,* the three men embarked upon their subterranean quest. "As I stepped on the first rung of the ladder," recalled Thompson, "each of the pumping gang, my faithful native boys, left his place in turn and with a very solemn face shook hands with me and then went back again to wait for the signal. It was not hard to read their thoughts. They were bidding me a last farewell, never expecting to see me again. Then, releasing my hold on the ladder, I sank like a bag of lead, leaving behind me a silvery trail of bubbles."

He watched the water change from amber to green and finally to an impenetrable black. His submarine flashlight was powerless to penetrate the veil of darkness in which he was shrouded. He groped blindly along the floor until he located a ledge or crevice, then sifted its contents by hand. Here and there were steep mud walls, laden with rocks and tree trunks, which had escaped the jaws of the dredge. These proved to be a dangerous hazard, for, as Thompson explained, "every

little while one of the stone blocks, loosened from its place in
the wall by the infiltration of the water, would come plunging
down upon us in the worse than Stygian darkness that was all
about us."

For several weeks the divers made daily sojourns to the
bottom of the well. The Indians, who watched the proceedings
with abject fascination, waited for the terrible consequence
they were certain would come about: outraged gods lurking
in some unseen cavern beneath the surface would surely
pounce upon them and drag them to a watery grave. But no
serious mishaps detracted from the copious rewards of their
efforts. Each time a diver reappeared from the depths his
pouch brimmed with new discoveries—pieces of carved jade,
objects of gold and copper, sculptured stones, and human remains. Among the treasures recovered were several superbly
fashioned ceremonial knives of the type used to cut the heart
from the breast of sacrificial victims. One of these was
wrought of finely worked flint, and its handle was of carved
wood in the form of two entwined serpents overlaid with gold.
Of the identifiable skeletons, twenty-one were children between the ages of eighteen months and twelve years; thirteen
were men and eight were women.

Almost all of the artifacts recovered from the *cenote*
seemed to have been deliberately broken. Thompson was of
the opinion that the Maya had adhered to the widespread
tradition among ancient peoples of "killing" objects intended
as votive offerings—smashing them so that their "spirits"
might accompany the deceased with whom they were entombed. Most authorities concur with his assumption: objects
of art—like offerings of human life—were intended as gifts
from the multitudes to their divine patrons. Only by a ceremonial death, destruction at the hands of priests, could their
spirit be so conveyed.

Thompson's findings left no area of reasonable doubt that

the Sacred Cenote had indeed been the scene of human sacrifices carried out in the manner described by Landa and
Figueroa. But his almost half-century of exploration at
Chichén Itzá ended with a series of unfortunate occurrences.
During the years from 1910 to 1930 Yucatán was ravaged by
political upheavals and open revolutions. On one such occasion
the hacienda in which Thompson had lived and established his
laboratory was burned and totally destroyed. Lost beyond
reclamation was his valuable library on Mayan antiquities, as
well as many of the priceless specimens recovered from the
ruins. Later the hacienda was rebuilt and leased to the
Carnegie Institution of Washington as headquarters for their
extensive program of excavation and research at Chichén
Itzá.

Subsequent legal difficulties then developed between Thompson and the Mexican government over the rumored value of
the objects reclaimed from the Sacred Well. Some estimates
placed the monetary worth of the "Thompson treasure" as
high as $500,000. He steadfastly maintained such appraisals
to be "fantastic and extravagant," and pointed out that its
value could be arrived at only in terms of the worth of his
findings to scientific research. But the Mexican government
did not concur with his approach to the matter; objects of
gold, they retorted, had a fixed market value, especially those
of ancient origin. As the collection had been removed by
Thompson for safekeeping at Harvard's Peabody Museum,
his property in Yucatán was confiscated and held against pay-
ment of roughly half a million dollars. He was forced to
relinquish his ownership of the plantation and forsake plans
for future excavations at Chichén Itzá.

"...I should have been false to my duty as an archaeologist," he wrote in his defense, "had I, believing that the scientific treasures were at the bottom of the Sacred Well, failed
to improve the opportunity and attempt to bring them to

light, thus making them available for scientific study . . . I should have been equally false to my duty as a scientist if . . . I had neglected to take all possible measures for their immediate security and permanent safety."

The abundance of material reclaimed by Thompson from the Well of Sacrifice indicated that offerings of human life had taken place there with ominous regularity. And because of the pronounced necessity for sacrifices in Toltec religion, many scholars were inclined to believe that the ritualistic use of the well had not come about until sometime after the Itzá occupation of Yucatán.

Recent studies have thrown a shadow of doubt on this assumption. Some of the carved jades from the depths of the well are unquestionably of Classic period workmanship. One, carved at Piedras Negras, was inscribed with the date A.D. 706, and another, almost surely from Palenque, bore an inscription of A.D. 690. Archaeologists were forced to ask themselves whether these jades indicated that pilgrimages from such distant centers had journeyed to the Well of Sacrifice as early as the seventh and eighth centuries, or had these objects been kept through the years, perhaps as closely guarded heirlooms, and cast into the well at some later date?

But the pyramid that contained the graves and the high priest's sepulcher was clearly of Toltec origin. Its serpentine balustrades represented the mighty Kukulcan, and the practice of killing slaves or lesser priests and entombing them with a person of higher rank was intimately associated with Toltec customs. Thompson's findings had added still more confirmation to what the archaeologists of his day had already begun to suspect: that the mark of Toltec culture was deeply imprinted upon the great Mayan metropolis of Chichén Itzá.

In choosing to explore the Well of Sacrifice, Edward Thompson had joined that select minority of antiquarians who, by discoveries of a startling and indisputable nature, were able to establish the authenticity of long-ignored myths and literary accounts drawn from folklore. He resides with such titans of archaeological fame as Heinrich Schliemann, who had meticulously pursued Homer's Troy to the plains of Hissarlik and there uncovered the site of the Greek historian's heroic epic; and John Lloyd Stephens, whose insatiable curiosity concerning the maligned cities of the Maya had made him the father of the science to which Thompson had devoted his life.

CHAPTER 13

Warfare, Disunity, and Decline: The Mayan "Dark Age"

BY the year A.D. 1200, the northern half of the Yucatán Peninsula had bowed to the stringent domination of the Itzás. Its leading cities—Uxmal, Kabah, Sayil, and Labná— had been abandoned. Elsewhere a few religious centers were kept alive by struggling priesthoods. Of the major cities, Chichén Itzá alone continued to flourish as before under the fresh stimulation of Itzá occupation.

The Mayan populace had not found it possible to recover from the mysterious weaknesses which had brought about the collapse of their age-old traditions and deprived them of their intellectual gifts; the Itzá conquest had come swiftly to subdue their sovereignty and alter their independent destiny.

From the twelfth century onward until the Spanish conquest, the sequence of events in Yucatán was obscured in a mist of fragmentary evidence gleaned from sources of doubtful reliability. It was unlikely that Chichén Itzá had remained the only large urban center; in fact, there were indications that it had slowly been abandoned in the years following A.D. 1200. And there were still numerous ruins in northern Yucatán about which nothing was known archaeologically, although they figured prominently in native accounts.

One such place reappeared frequently in post-Conquest documents—that of a once-populous city known as Mayapán, a sprawling maze of debris-littered mounds located some thirty miles south of Merída. For years it had remained a paradox. It was often mentioned in the *Books of Chilam Balam* and the narratives of Bishop Landa, but archaeologists had not undertaken to validate its history.

Native chronicles attributed to Mayapán an important role during the concluding years of Mayan history. It was here, so these sources related, that the Itzás, under the supervision of the mighty Kukulcan, had founded a new capital following the dissolution of Chichén Itzá. Here, too, a powerful ruling lord named Hunac Ceel was said to have established the seat of a dictatorship which eventually brought all of Yucatán under its jurisdiction.

Landa gives the following account of the city's origin:

> This Kukulcan established another city after arranging with the native lords of the country that he and they should live there and that all their affairs and business should be brought there; and for this purpose they chose a very good situation, eight leagues further in the interior than Merída is now, and fifteen or sixteen leagues from the sea. They surrounded it with a very broad stone wall ... leaving in it only two narrow gates. The wall was not very high and in the midst of this enclosure they built their temples, and the largest, which is like that of Chichén Itzá, they called Kukulcan, and they built another of a round form, with four doors, entirely different from all the others in that land.... In this enclosure they built houses for the lords only, dividing all the land among them, giving a town to each one, according to the antiquity of his lineage and his personal value. And Kukulcan gave a name to this city—not his own name as the Ah Itzás had done in Chichén Itzá, which means the well of the Ah Itzás, but he called it Mayapán, which means 'the standard of the Maya.'... Kukulcan lived with the lords in that city for several years; and leaving them in great peace and friendship, he returned by the same way to Mexico,

and on the way he stopped at Champoton, and, in memory
of him and his departure, he erected a fine building in
the sea like that of Chichén Itzá, a long stone's throw
from the shore. And thus Kukulcan left a perpetual remembrance in Yucatán.

Again scholars were faced with a familiar problem—that
of determining the validity of folklore in reconstructing
historical facts. However, preliminary investigations seemed
to bear out certain essential details of Landa's text: the vast
city of Mayapán *was* enclosed within the confines of a stone
wall, and its principal ceremonial structures were clustered
around a pyramid-temple similar in many respects to the Temple of Kukulcan at Chichén Itzá. But there was much more
to the native accounts concerning Mayapán.

Supposedly Yucatán was governed for some two hundred
years by a "triple alliance" consisting of the three most influential centers of the northern peninsula: Chichén Itzá, Uxmal,
and Mayapán. Historically the dates ascribed to the epochal
political union fall approximately between A.D. 987 and 1194,
varying according to discrepancies encountered in conflicting
versions of its history. It was said that this League of Mayapán, as it was called, brought about a degree of stability
during the troubled interim in which the manifestations newly
introduced by the Itzás were implanted among older Mayan
traditions. Ostensibly, the reins of temporal power over the
entire territory were held jointly by lords representing each
of the League's three member cities. Ultimately, however,
political frictions touched off intrigue and open revolt, resulting in a shattering upheaval which was to topple the League
of Mayapán and provide the background for an obscure noble
to seize singlehanded control of Yucatán.

But archaeological findings have failed to bear out this historical outline as portrayed in existing chronicles. Excavations
carried out by the Mexican government have disclosed that

Uxmal did not support a heavy or continuous population during the two centuries that the League of Mayapán reportedly
ruled Yucatán; in all probability its population diminished
along with the other great centers late in the ninth century.
What's more, it has been demonstrated that Mayapán
emerged as a city of importance only after Chichén Itzá had
lost its place of eminence as the peninsula's leading center
near the close of the twelfth century. Thus, as J. Eric Thompson, George Brainerd, Alberto Ruz, and others have pointed
out, the three cities said to have comprised the ruling triumvirate did not flourish simultaneously, at least not during the
entire two hundred years of the League's supposed ascendancy.
However, it is not impossible that some such federation had
exercised a system of mutual control over the northern portion
of the peninsula during the period in question, and that inac-
curate accounts of its structure gave rise to the discrepancies
in its history. Whatever the facts may ultimately prove to
be, the native versions of the League's bloody dissolution
bring us to a fascinating juncture—the so-called "plot of
Hunac Ceel." If the essence of this account can be accepted
in its literal translation, then we encounter one of the most
significant dramas in the whole sweeping panorama of Mayan
affairs.

According to what can be inferred from the vague narratives dealing with his rise to prominence—principally those
contained in the *Books of Chilam Balam*—Hunac Ceel had
grown alarmed at the complacency with which the provinces
were being governed by the surviving regime of the League of
Mayapán. He was especially distrustful of the ruling lords of
Chichén Itzá whose authority apparently bordered upon despotism. It was while witnessing the enactment of a sacrifice at
the Sacred Well that Hunac resolved to alter the declining fortunes of his people. He must have felt strangely apprehensive
as he watched the procession of *chilanes* leading the captives

from the Temple of Kukulcan along the stone-coated avenue toward the Sacred Well. Solemnly they entered the clearing and ascended the platform at the well's edge. Hovering around the well, and for some distance in all directions, was a sea of peasant faces beneath a streaming canopy of banners and sacred emblems. The captives stood as though numbed by the reality of death. Some minutes later they had one by one been dragged forward, anointed, laden with ornaments of gold and jade, and cast down into the green water.

Then there was silence. And throughout the hot morning they waited tensely at the pool's edge for the sun to reach its noon zenith—to see if by then any of the sacrifices remained alive to bear messages from the spirits below.

When the midday sun hung directly overhead, the water's green surface was unbroken by stirrings of life. Not one among the captives remained to tell of his divine concourse. The future of those who waited above was now a matter of faith. Perhaps there was impiety in Hunac Ceel's nature; or perhaps he recognized that "faith" had come to signify the absolute acceptance of the whims and corruption of the ruling lords. This was Hunac's supreme opportunity.

He dashed forward from the retinue of nobles, mounted the temple platform, and, before the startled crowd, threw himself into the waiting mouth of the well! Moments later the jade water broke into white foam as he emerged to proclaim that he himself had spoken with the gods, and by their own words he—Hunac Ceel—had been affirmed as their ruler.

Hunac's courage ignited the onlooking crowd and cries of support arose for the young lord. He was brought up from the well and extolled by them as their leader!

Intense, indeed, must have been the drama of that moment, when, for the first time in Mayan history, one man seized the helm of the entire empire. Hunac Ceel's ascendancy was to spell doom for the existing triumvirate of city-states. He selected Mayapán as the sole capital of his authority, and established, under the title of his family name, the house of Cocom. Lords faithful to his cause assumed the duties of provincial administrators, and they were required to govern from Mayapán where Hunac could personally supervise their policies and guard their allegiances.

But the displaced lords of Chichén Itzá, who had now yielded their temporal powers to Hunac Ceel, were not easily pacified. Hunac was uncertain of the loyalty of his emissaries there, especially its appointed regent, Chac Xib Chac. He looked about for a means of ridding himself of this worrisome threat to his unchallenged domination of Yucatán. Exactly how this was accomplished is again clouded by various conflicting accounts, but an intriguing reference in the *Books of Chilam Balam* would have us believe that Hunac Ceel employed the subtleties of political intrigue to further his lordly ambitions. Eventually war was presaged by Hunac against Chichén Itzá, according to this account, in his efforts to rescue the bride of an ally who had been abducted by the untrustworthy Chac Xib Chac. Other versions differ as to the motives underlying the conflict, but so devastating was the destruction wrought by Hunac's legions that Chichén Itzá—once the brightest jewel in the Maya-Itzá crown—was thereafter abandoned to ruin. Activity gradually diminished at the former Itzá capital from the end of the twelfth century onward; most of its lofty structures lay in ruins when Montejo's army took refuge amid its crumbled grandeurs four hundred years later. Its captive lords, so say the chronicles, were brought to Mayapán and installed as provisional emissaries of the Cocoms.

From this point on, Mayapán became the most powerful city in the peninsula; its armies were swelled by professional soldiers recruited from Tabasco—fierce Mexican warriors known as the Ah Canul whose devotion to the Cocoms was purchased by guarantees of prestige and the spoils of military victories. Surrounded by a walled city, garrisoned by an army beholden only to himself, Hunac Ceel founded a dynasty that was to hold the reins of political authority over Yucatán for two hundred and fifty years.

But the Cocom inheritance was pre-emptive and often abusive, even to supposedly favored chieftains. Jealousy and intrigue—the inevitable fissures in a corrupting regime—eventually began to shatter the Cocoms' influence upon subordinate lords. Once the weaknesses became apparent, the waiting malefactors seized their "moments of destiny" as Hunac himself had done two and a half centuries earlier. Resentment grew against the Cocom leadership at Mayapán, until the partisans of one Tutul Xiu—a descendant of Uxmal's former ruling house—joined in a plot to overthrow the now oppressive regime. "This they did," writes Bishop Landa, "killing at the same time all of his sons save one who was absent; they sacked his dwelling and possessed themselves of all his property ... saying that thus they repaid themselves what had been stolen from them." Various other accounts bear out that Mayapán was besieged and set afire by an army under the command of Tutul Xiu in the year 1441. Mayan history had arrived at the ultimate substratum of its decline—total anarchy!

Such was the relatively brief but significant outline of Mayapán's history as gleaned from the writings of native and Spanish chroniclers. It bespoke of a curious pattern of events and manifestations wholly foreign to long-established traditions: walled cities, governing confederations, large-scale warfare, and political intrigue. But how much could be accepted as representative of actual occurrences? Its chronological sequence was desultory and confusing; its fragmentary details suggested that they may have been drawn as much from spurious legends as accurate recollection. Archaeologists confronted an immense problem in their efforts to discern the truth of Mayapán's lineage. It was not likely that the whole story would be reclaimed from its rubble: the descent of ruling houses and the complexities of political manipulations are seldom recovered from the earth unless they are recorded on imperishable substances in a decipherable script. So far no inscriptions have been found which would seem to bear upon such matters, yet that alone does not preclude the possibility that texts of this kind will eventually come to light. Also there is the obstacle of the hieroglyphs that cannot be understood, and the fact that the greatest potential store of pre-Conquest documents which might conceivably have borne on this question—the library at Mani— was lost to modern science by the fanaticism of Diego de Landa. Had those priceless codices been preserved and their hieroglyphic texts deciphered, specific persons and events in Mayan history might well be as familiar to us as the personalities and deeds of Caesar, Attila, Charlemagne, or Peter the Great.

Obviously, however, Mayapán's enormous size, its unique ground plan, and prominent role in existing documents merited further investigation. Utilizing these facts as a point of departure, a team of archaeologists from the Carnegie Institution set out to reclaim the city's principal structures from their shroud of debris and underbrush. It was discovered that the site was even larger than had been previously supposed; over three thousand five hundred buildings of various types were mapped within the confines of its walls. Out of the mounting evidence exhumed by excavation there emerged possible indications that the city might indeed have witnessed events suggestive of those attributed to it by native historians.

George Brainerd wrote that Mayapán's "gateways show careful planning against military attack. Within the wall was a religious precinct, as described by Landa, although the low, secondary wall said to have surrounded it has not been located. ... Around the temples of the major centers were grouped colonnaded rectangular buildings with solid rear walls, which probably represent the official quarters of the regional kings. . . . These buildings face upon a series of paved plazas. . . .

"Throughout the town are irregularly spaced houses, most of which were at least partially of masonry construction. When available, slightly elevated ground was chosen for their location, presumably for reasons of drainage, which is always a problem in Yucatán during heavy rains. Low dry-stone property walls surround these houses, enclosing irregularly shaped dooryards. . . . Meandering among the haphazardly placed houses are lanes or passages of a sort, their irregular boundaries fixed by whatever property walls chance to be adjacent. . . ."

New types of artifacts were also unearthed, including a number of ornate effigy urns of molded ceramics which had originally been painted with garish colors. Of particular interest was the presence of finely worked arrowheads which almost surely indicated that the bow and arrow—previously unknown to the Maya—had come into the possession of Mayapán's armies.

Each new structure laid bare reaffirmed the seal of Itzá influence upon Mayapán. It appeared everywhere in the form of the familiar serpentine columns, circular structures, the extensive use of colonnades, and sculptural motifs that reflect the influence of Mexican ideals as lucidly as those found at Chichén Itzá. But one notable difference distinguished Mayapán from the usual Mayan city: numerous structures were uncovered within its walls which appeared to have been erected solely as dwelling places. Often they were arranged along alleyways and were subdivided into crowded quarters as though priests, nobles, soldiers, and the peasant population—previously segregated strata of society—had dwelled together for reasons of mutual defense.

Although the site had been sparsely occupied for a considerable length of time, its most imposing structures had been

erected *after* Chichén Itzá reached its zenith late in the twelfth
century. Its peculiar fortress-like features were almost surely
inspired by the Cocom's predilection for war, and the rectangular buildings clustered near its important temples may, as
Brainerd suggested, have housed the regional lords brought to
Mayapán from subordinate provinces by Hunac Ceel and his
Cocom successors. And there were positive indications that the
city's greatness had ended in fire-ridden violence, though
whether wrought by the legions of Tutul Xiu as the chronicles
related can only be guessed.

A summary view of the findings yielded by Mayapán reflects
the chaotic spectacle of a once brilliant civilization on the brink
of disaster : a walled refuge garrisoned by mercenary troops, its
supremacy maintained by force of arms, its arts and crafts in
sharp decline, ruled by lords less in awe of their gods than the
glories of military might, its governing councils filled with the
displaced nobles of subjugated districts—puppets in function
and political hostages in reality. Grievous indeed were these
mutations which had misdirected the Maya so far from the
values and attainments of their forebears. How had they occurred among a people whose traditions were rooted in
aesthetic pursuits of the highest order?

Very likely there were a number of contributing factors
inspired primarily by the initial collapse of Classic culture, and
the imposition of wholly alien ideologies by the Itzás in the
wake of these shattering events. J. Eric Thompson, in *The Rise
and Fall of Maya Civilization,* reviewing the traumatic state
of affairs evidenced in Mayapán's ruins, draws particularly
significant conclusions regarding the corrosive effect of Itzá
religious manifestations in explaining the dissolution of Mayan
ethics or morals. For with the Toltec colonists who invaded
Yucatán there came their fierce, warlike gods, who eventually
displaced or aborted the old and venerable deities whose
infinite mysteries had so long cloaked the Mayan peasant in

humble servitude. Veneration of the more sanguinary Mexican gods necessitated human sacrifices on a scale never conceived by the Maya until their subjects found themselves forced to wage war in order to satisfy spiritual needs. Slowly by the mixture of Mayan and Itzá blood there arose a new generation that willingly exchanged the dim legacy of an effaced heritage for the boldly conceived promises of the more rigorous Itzá gods, the patrons of war, fire, sacrifice, and the sun whose covenant promised: *Feed us well upon the blood of captives and you shall be justly rewarded.*

Once unleashed, concluded Thompson, the esoteric inspiration of such militant tendencies was inevitably distorted. Eventually the adoration of warrior gods begot a society in which the soldier usurped the temporal powers formerly held by priests. It was then but a brief step until the Maya found themselves hopelessly involved in a wave of petty wars and internecine strife. Mayan youths began to taste of a glory unknown to their ancestors—an exultant, physical glory extracted from the clash of arms and the prestige of conquest. It was a perverse elation that was to consign their destiny as a civilization to oblivion. How like that of the last days of pharaonic Egypt and imperial Rome was this psychosis with which the Maya were now afflicted. And how suggestive of the dilemma inherited by the twentieth century!

Whatever the full range of causes underlying the abrupt distortion of their ideals, the civilizing factors inherent among the Maya from their earliest beginnings ended with the violent demission of Mayapán. What happened thereafter—in the years following its alleged destruction by the Tutul Xius in 1441—must again be inferred from early narratives which provide only fragmentary glimpses into the troubled times which descended upon Yucatán. We read that only one Cocom lord had survived the fall of their former capital; he led the remnants of his followers away from the plundered city and

founded a new settlement known as Tibolon. The Ah Canul—
the professional warriors hired by the Cocoms as personal
guards—were banished to the northwestern corner of the
peninsula. Long before, many of Chichén Itzá's former inhabitants, fleeing the wrath of Hunac Ceel, had migrated southward into the heart of the Petén forest where they erected an
island garrison known as Tayasal on Lake Petén. And the victorious Tutul Xiu lords established a new capital at Mani,
seventy miles southeast of Chichén Itzá. Ironically the word
mani signified: "it is finished."

No single chieftain possessed the military might to reor-
ganize and unify the far-flung provinces which now separated
Yucatán into a series of antagonistic armed camps. But as
numerous lords entertained ambitions of bringing about such
a unification under their dominion, the stage was readied for
a chaotic denouement! Open warfare erupted throughout the
peninsula. Villages were raided for their yield of sacrificial
victims and youths suitable for military conscription. Often
raiders, striking at night, would set fire to outlying milpas in
order to starve villages into submission to a covetous lord. One
after another, petty kings rose and fell, usually displaced by
betrayal or outright assassination. Life was worth the meager-
est of prices; attempts to preserve former traditions were
gradually abandoned. Virtually all of the ceremonial centers
were desolate, art and science were no longer pursued, intellectual strivings had ceased.

At no time thereafter was the memory resurrected of the
golden age that must surely have lurked in folklore, legend,
and the pristine temples lying about in ruins. There was no
renaissance of creative expression; no emissaries of common
sense; none to challenge the farcicality of their militaristic
gods, or the egocentric crusades by which they were cajoled into
warfare. After four centuries of existence by the sword it had

become a way of life, the means of material gain, the synonym for security. And the prophets of disaster went unheard. . . .

Armed camps, pillaging, disunity, economic exhaustion, and moral decay had taken their toll: the Maya had no time remaining in which to resolve the lamentable state of their affairs.

It was now the early spring of 1517. The ships of Hernández de Córdoba were drawing within sight of Yucatán; the Mayan sentry had alerted his chieftain to their presence. With his retinue of nobles he went to the water's edge to view for himself the curious mountains risen out of the sea on clouds, remembering that the prophets of Chilam Balam had forewarned of such happenings:

> *On that day, a blight is on the face of the earth,*
> *On that day, a cloud rises,*
> *On that day, a strong man seizes the land,*
> *On that day, things fall to ruin.*

A meeting was held among the chiefs. Later they went forth in longboats to counsel with the emissaries of Charles the Fifth, the Emperor of Spain, the "strongest man of his day."

Uxmal

One of the fascinating aspects of archaeology is the treading back along the developmental path of various civilizations. We journey in reverse from the end to the means—from the visible culmination of historical epochs to their obscure origins—and thus gain new perspective and a fresh objectivity. Always there are voids that can be bridged only by intelligent speculation, but persistent research along varied routes of approach will eventually supply an accurate outline of occurrences.

Arnold Toynbee has written: "Actuality is less important than man's aspirations which are best expressed in artistic creativity." By this axiom the Maya of the Classic empire had achieved their eminent status among the civilizations of the ancient world. One has only to examine against the background of recognizable history the vigorous sculpture of Copán, or walk among the sedate structures of Palenque, to comprehend the incipient tenure of Mayan aspirations—the harmonious union of man with the dark powers of creation, human experience with spiritual mysticism. One fact then becomes obvious here as everywhere else in antiquity: the Maya were attuned to the universal theme of civilization—man in relation to the unknown. So long as this quest—this exploration of the ethos— remained uppermost in their endeavors, the fortunes of the Maya continued skyward.

What was it, then, that altered their moderate way of life and opened the way for the emergence of disastrous influences? Never has it been possible to attribute the decline of a civilization to any single cause. But certain weaknesses were inherent within Mayan culture from its inception, and each of them has been suggested as contributing in some measure to its eventual destruction.

Scholars took particular note of the fact that the Mayan system of agriculture—the most important single ingredient in their development—remained relatively primitive throughout their history; they were without the advantages of irrigation, crop rotation, and the variety of implements usually associated with agricultural endeavors. Furthermore, the milpa system required a widely scattered population and an almost constant expenditure of effort to hold back the jungle.

Their environmental surroundings were extremely discouraging if present-day conditions are a reliable indication of the severity of the heat, humidity, and density of the forested lands in which Mayan civilization had its birth and progressive development. Yet these circumstances were perhaps not so much a disadvantage as a challenge to their ingenuity, a stimulation brought about by necessity and the precariousness of their situation. The Maya seemed to have come to terms with these external detriments; in spite of them were born their brilliant accomplishments in astronomy, mathematics, hieroglyphics, architecture, and sculpture.

We are also reminded that their technology remained conspicuously underdeveloped; it was upon this important consideration that Sylvanus Morley based his over-all evaluation of Mayan civilization: *

> In his long, arduous journey forward from savagery to a civilized state, the first five steps by which man has advanced are generally admitted to be the following: control of fire, invention of agriculture, domestication of animals, tools of metal, and discovery of the principle of the wheel. The sequence of these successive steps is not always given in the same order and was not always the same in different parts of the world, though control of fire was undoubtedly the first everywhere and the invention of agriculture probably the second in most places, the order of the remaining three steps varying.
>
> What was the cultural scratch of the ancient Maya with respect to these five basic steps of human advancement? It goes without saying that they had mastered fire, had learned how to make and preserve it. We have seen . . . that they had developed an admirable system of agriculture . . . in view of the relatively unfavorable nature of their region. . . .
>
> It is true that the Maya had domesticated the wild turkey and kept swarms of wild, stingless bees in special

* Reprinted from *The Ancient Maya,* by Sylvanus G. Morley, with the permission of the publishers, Stanford University Press. Copyright 1946, 1947, and 1956 by the Board of Trustees of Leland Stanford Junior University.

thatched huts near their homes, but they had not one of the
beasts of burden which so tremendously helped man in the
Old World. Indeed, in all America there would seem to
have been but two examples of the use of beasts of burden
in pre-Columbian times—the llama used as a pack animal
by the ancient Peruvians and the dog used by the Eskimo
to haul their sleds. All of the tremendous building program
of the ancient Maya was accomplished without the aid of a
single carrying animal other than man himself. . . .

There were no metal tools. Metal . . . was non-existent
in the Old Empire; and in the New Empire [now referred
to as the Mexican period] gold and copper and their alloys
were used exclusively in making articles of personal adorn-
ment, or for ceremonial use such as rings, beads, pendants,
ear-plugs, bells, cups, plates, plaques, and the like.

The principle of the wheel was unknown to the ancient
Maya. They had no wheeled vehicles of any kind . . . and
most students of aboriginal American ceramics are agreed
that the potter's wheel for turning pottery was also unknown. . . . In short, the Maya were acquainted with and
enjoyed the use of only the first two of the foregoing five
"steps toward civilization."

The ancient Egyptians, Chaldeans, Babylonians, Assyri-
ans, Persians, Chinese, Phoenicians, Etruscans, Greeks, and
Romans possessed all five of these aids to civilization. The
Khmers of Cambodia and the builders of the great rock-cut
temples of Java were the only other people beside the Maya
who developed early, high civilizations in the wet tropics,
but they too made daily use of these five primary aids to
human progress. Indeed, in order to find a condition in the
Old World comparable to the Maya cultural scratch as
just established, it is necessary to go far back in human history, far beyond any of the civilizations just mentioned, to
early Neolithic times—the Age of Polished Stone when
man's knowledge and utensils were similarly restricted. On
this primitive horizon, and on this alone, may the Maya
civilization be fairly compared with the prehistoric civilizations of the Old World. And if this comparison be made,
it will be found that, starting from the same cultural

scratch, no Neolithic people of the Old World ever reached such heights of achievement as did the ancient Maya of Middle America.

Undoubtedly it is to the less obvious weaknesses that we must look if the riddle of the Mayan collapse is ever to be fully understood, especially to the recurring question of the populace in relation to their priestly overlords. Having once brought about an orderly progression of their society—with the peasants and the hierarchy each carrying out functions necessary to the support of the other—it is probable that the priesthoods began to take for granted their control over the populace. Eventually, religion became concerned with matters unrelated to the focal point of mass fear and piety—the gods of the soil. It soared into purely esoteric realms until it lost contact with the peasants upon whose continuing support the priesthoods depended.

Subsequent discoveries at Tikal have led to speculation that some manner of civil unrest may have plagued the Maya far longer than was at first indicated. Stelae dating from the *middle* of the Classic period were recently uncovered which appear to have been intentionally smashed after the fashion of the religious objects found at Piedras Negras and in later horizons at Tikal. While it is too early to evaluate the full significance of these findings, it may well be that the peasants were even then growing dubious of the burdens placed upon them by their priests. Or such evidence might have resulted from conflicting factions within the hierarchy itself. Whatever caused the Old Empire to crumble—leaving its magnificent cities to the jungle and its intellectual heritage to a disillusioned, illiterate multitude—Mayan civilization entered a decline from which it never again emerged.

We have seen how the past century and a half brought Mayan archaeology forward from the limbo of skepticism and occult theorizing into the light of factual reconstruction and soundly based conjecture. Yet before archaeologists whose efforts have thus far revealed so much, there remains a vast sea of mystery. Many of the initial problems that confronted investigators of a century ago are still unresolved. Much remains to be learned concerning the evolution of Mayan civilization

Uxmal

out of the Archaic horizon in Middle America. It is still not known exactly where in the pattern of early migrations the Mayoid tribes first assembled, or when, precisely, they settled in their tropical homeland. We can only hypothesize as to how and when the calendar and hieroglyphic writing made their appearance as dominating factors in Mayan development. Fully two thirds of their hieroglyphic script have yet to be deciphered and the presently meaningless inscriptions fitted into existing knowledge. There is virtually no information bearing upon the government of the city-states and their interrelationship in matters of trade and politics. Nor can we yet be certain of the conspiracy of events underlying the collapse of the Old Empire at the very height of its florescence. It remains an enigma without parallel in world history. Unlike the often-repeated rise and fall of modern and archaic empires—the recurrent theme of mankind's efforts to formulate an ideal state—Mayan civilization was started on its downward path by its own hand! Why? It is possible that we may never know.

A great deal concerning the Mexican period is still to be explained: the full story of the Itzás and the avenues by which they found their way into Yucatán, the source of the Quetzal-coatl-Kukulcan myth, and the entire intriguing panorama of petty lords and ruling dynasties whose conflicts left the Maya unprepared for the threat of Spanish invasion.

In 1956 Tulane University's Middle American Research Institute began unearthing a series of badly weathered mounds at a site known as Dzibilchaltun near Mérida, Yucatán. Under the direction of E. Wyllys Andrews the work accomplished thus far has produced startling results: It was soon discovered that this previously unrecorded city was perhaps the largest ever erected by the ancient Maya; its ruins cover more than twenty square miles. Of even greater significance is the fact that the levels of occupation at Dzibilchaltun extend continuously from early pre-Classic times—perhaps as remote as 2000 B.C. —until well *after* the colonization of Yucatán by the Spanish. Thus it appears to have been inhabited during each of the stages incident to the rise and fall of Mayan culture, witnessing its birth out of Archaic backgrounds, the florescence and mysterious collapse of its brilliant achievements, and the troubled centuries before and after the Conquest. Realizing the potential importance of Dzibilchaltun in establishing an unbroken sequence of events in Yucatán, the National Geographic Society recently joined in the efforts to reconstruct its history.

Far to the south in the Petén forest, archaeologists of the University of Pennsylvania Museum, directed by Edwin Shook, are laboring to excavate and restore the imposing structures of Tikal. It is a monumental undertaking: an airfield had to be opened to permit the delivery of water and supplies, and a permanent camp and laboratory erected to house the field staff during the estimated ten years required to complete the project.

In the lowlands of the Usumacinta and its tributaries, Harvard's Peabody Museum is conducting extensive reconnaissance and excavation; and Kaminaljuyú—an important site in the highlands of Guatemala—is undergoing a long-range program of excavation and partial restoration.

When will it be that an explorer, a chicle gatherer, or perhaps a mining engineer will next stumble upon an astonishing discovery—new reflections of the genius that was the keynote of Mayan evolution; a guide by which the full range of glyphic writing can be deciphered; a graphic pictorialization of the events underlying the submission of the Old Empire—murals or hieroglyphic codices; unsuspected routes of trade with outside areas, or revelations concerning the identity of Kukulcan? Momentarily an accidental discovery might well clarify the riddle of centuries.

Immense portions of the ancient Mayan kingdom remain unexplored. The waters of the Usumacinta River flow past uncounted numbers of their desolate cities which no scientist has yet freed from jungle growth and the rubble of decay. In the Petén forest and the central reaches of the Yucatán Peninsula lie a myriad overgrown temples and shattered acropolises; and the mountainous highlands of Guatemala and Honduras are dotted with mounds and half-exposed structures.

Like Stephens, Maudslay, Thompson, and Ruz, other men will probe these unknown tracts until their secrets are finally reclaimed. The lure of such things is irresistible.

A BRIEF CHRONOLOGY OF THE SIGNIFICANT
EVENTS OF MAYAN HISTORY

(According to the Goodman-Hernández-Thompson correlation)

A.D.	320		The Leyden Plate: The earliest dated object recovered from the Mayan area.
	328		Stela 9, Uaxactún: The earliest dated monument recovered from the Mayan area.
	357		Stelae 18 and 19, Uaxactún: The first monuments erected to commemorate Katun endings in Mayan chronology.
	416		Stela 18, Tikal: The earliest known monument from the largest Classic city.
	475		The earliest date recorded in the northern Yucatán Peninsula. Oxkintok, Yucatán.
	545		An astronomical conference held at Copán to correlate calendrical innovations.
	790	(?)	The Bonampak murals painted.
	800		Stela cult abandoned at Copán; beginning of Classic decline.
	889		Date of last stelae from the Classic period.
	909		Latest surely dated object from the Classic period: A jade gorget, Tzibanche, Quintana Roo.
	987		The settling of Mayapán by the Itzás.
	987 to 1185	(?)	The League of Mayapán.
	1194		Rise of Hunac Ceel: The fall of Chichén Itzá.
	1204 to 1140		The ascendancy of Mayapán.
	1441		The destruction of Mayapán by the Xius: End of centralized authority.
	1464		Hurricane strikes Yucatán.
	1480		Plague.
	1517		Córdoba lands on coast of Yucatán.
	1542		Founding of Mérida.
	1697		Tayasal, the last capital of the Itzás, is conquered by the Spanish.

Bibliography

ACOSTA, JORGE R. "Exploraciones en Tula, Hidalgo," *Revista Mexicana de Estudios Antropológicos* (Mexico), Vol. 4, No. 3 (1940).

ANDREWS, E. WYLLYS. "Dzibilchaltun: Lost City of the Maya," *National Geographic* Magazine, January, 1959.

BLOM, FRANZ. *The Conquest of Yucatán.* Boston: Houghton Mifflin Company, 1936.

———— and LAFARGE, OLIVER. *Tribes and Temples.* ("Middle American Research Series," No. 1.) New Orleans: Tulane University, 1926.

BOURBOURG, ABBÉ BRASSEUR DE. *Histoire des nations civilisées du Mexique et de l'Amérique Centrale.* Paris, 1857-59.

BRAINERD, GEORGE W. *The Maya Civilization.* Los Angeles: Southwest Museum, 1954.

BRINTON, D. G. *The Annals of the Cakchiquels.* The Original Text, with a Translation, Notes, and Introduction. ("Brinton's Library of Aboriginal American Literature," No. 6.) Philadelphia, 1885.

————. *The Maya Chronicles.* ("Brinton's Library of Aboriginal American Literature," No. 1.) Philadelphia, 1882.

CATHERWOOD, F. *Views of Ancient Monuments in Central America, Chiapas, and Yucatán.* New York, 1844.

CHARNAY, DÉSIRÉ. *The Ancient Cities of the New World.* New York: Harper and Brothers, 1887.

CHONAY, DIONISIO JOSÉ. *Title of the Lords of Totonicapán.* English version by Delia Goetz. Norman: University of Oklahoma Press, 1953.

COVARRUBIAS, MIGUEL. *Indian Art of Mexico and Central America.* New York: Alfred A. Knopf, Inc., 1957.

DÍAZ DEL CASTILLO, BERNAL. *The Discovery and Conquest of Mexico.* Translated by A. P. Maudslay. Mexico City: The Mexico Press. New York: Farrar, Straus and Cudahy, Inc., 1956. London: Routledge & Kegan Paul, Ltd.

DONNELLY, IGNATIUS J. *Atlantis: The Antediluvian World*. New York: Harper and Brothers, 1882.

DUTTON, BERTHA P. "A Brief Discussion of Chichén Itzá," *El Palacio* (Santa Fe, New Mexico), Vol. 63 (1956).

———. "Tula of the Toltecs," *El Palacio* (Santa Fe, New Mexico), Vol. 62 (1955).

EKHOLM, GORDON. "Wheeled Toys in Mexico," *American Antiquity* (Andover), Vol. 2, No. 4 (1946).

FÖRSTEMANN, E. W. *Commentary on the Maya Manuscript in the Royal Library of Dresden*. ("Papers of the Peabody Museum of American Archaeology and Ethnology," Vol. IV, No. 2.) Cambridge: Harvard University, 1906.

GANN, T. W. F. *Maya Cities. A Record of Exploration and Adventure in Middle America*. London: Gerald Duckworth & Co., 1927. New York: Charles Scribner's Sons, 1928.

——— and THOMPSON, J. E. S. *The History of the Maya, from the Earliest Time to the Present Day*. New York: Charles Scribner's Sons, 1931.

GATES, WILLIAM. *An Outline Dictionary of Maya Glyphs*. ("Maya Society Publications," No. 1) Baltimore: Johns Hopkins Press, 1931.

GILPIN, LAURA. *Temples in Yucatán: A Camera Chronicle of Chichén Itzá*. New York: Hastings House, 1948.

GORDON, G. B. *Prehistoric Ruins of Copán, Honduras. A Preliminary Report of the Explorations by the Museum, 1891-95*. ("Memoirs of the Peabody Museum of American Archaeology and Ethnology," Vol. I, No. 1.) Cambridge: Harvard University, 1896.

HEWETT, EDGAR L. *Ancient Life in Mexico and Central America*. New York, 1943.

HIBBEN, FRANK C. *The Lost Americans*. New York: The Thomas Y. Crowell Company, 1947.

HOLMES, WILLIAM H. *Archaeological Studies among the Ancient Cities of Mexico*. Part I, Monuments of Yucatán; Part II, Monuments of Chiapas, Oaxaca and the Valley of Mexico. ("Anthropological Series," Vol. I.) Chicago: Field Columbian Museum, 1895.

IXTLILXOCHITL, FERNANDO DE ALVA. *Obras Históricas*. 2 vols. Mexico, 1891-92.

JAKEMAN, MAX WELLS. *The Origins and History of the Mayas.* Los Angeles: Research Publishing, 1945.

JOYCE, THOMAS ATHOL. *Maya and Mexican Art.* London, 1927.

KELEMAN, PÁL. *Medieval American Art.* 2 vols. New York, 1943.

KIDDER, A. V. *The Artifacts of Uaxactún, Guatemala.* ("Carnegie Institution of Washington Publication," No. 576.) Washington, D.C., 1947.

———, JENNINGS, J. D., and SHOOK, E. M. *Excavations at Kaminaljuyú, Guatemala.* ("Carnegie Institution of Washington Publication," No. 561.) Washington, D.C., 1946.

KROEBER, A. L. *Archaic Culture Horizons in the Valley of Mexico.* ("University of California Publications in American Archaeology and Ethnology.") Berkeley, 1925.

LANDA, DIEGO DE. *Relación de las cosas de Yucatán.* Madrid, 1881.

———. *Relación de las cosas de Yucatán,* Translation by Alfred M. Tozzer. ("Papers of the Peabody Museum of Archaeology and Ethnology," Vol. XVIII) Cambridge: Harvard University, 1941.

LAS CASAS, BARTOLOMÉ DE. *Apologética historia de las Indias.* ("Nueva Biblioteca de Autores Españoles. Historiadores de Indias," Vol. I.) Madrid, 1909.

LE PLONGEON, AUGUSTUS. *Sacred Mysteries among the Mayas and the Quiches: Their Relation to the Mysteries of Egypt, Greece, Chaldea, and India.* New York: Macoy Publishing and Masonic Supply Company, 1886.

LIBBY, WILLARD F. *Radiocarbon Dating.* Chicago: University of Chicago Press, 1955.

LOTHROP, S. K. *Metals from the Cenote of Sacrifice, Chichén Itzá, Yucatán.* ("Memoirs of the Peabody Museum of American Archaeology and Ethnology," Vol. X, No. 2.) Cambridge: Harvard University, 1952.

MACGOWAN, KENNETH. *Early Man in the New World.* New York: The Macmillan Company, 1950.

MALER, TEOBERT. *Explorations in the Department of Petén, Guatemala. Tikal. Report of Explorations for the Museum.* ("Memoirs of the Peabody Museum of American Archaeology and Ethnology," Vol. V, No. 1.) Cambridge: Harvard University, 1911.

MALER, TEOBERT. *Researches in the Central Portion of the Usumatsintla Valley. Report of Explorations for the Museum, 1898-1900.* ("Memoirs of the Peabody Museum of American Archaeology and Ethnology," Vol. V, No. 1.) Cambridge: Harvard University, 1901.

MARQUINA, I. *Arquitectura prehispánica.* Mexico: Instituto Nacional de Antropología e Historia, 1951.

MASON, GREGORY. *South of Yesterday.* New York: Henry Holt and Company, Inc., 1940.

MASON, J. A. *The American Collections of the University Museum: The Ancient Civilizations of Middle America.* University Museum Bulletin, Vol. X, Nos. 1-2, Philadelphia, 1943.

MAUDSLAY, A. P. *Archaeology, Biologia Centrali Americana.* 5 vols. London, 1889-1902.

The Maya and Their Neighbors. (Collection of essays) New York: D. Appleton-Century Company, 1940.

MEANS, P. A. *History of the Spanish Conquest of Yucatán and of the Itzás.* ("Papers of the Peabody Museum of American Archaeology and Ethnology," Vol. VII.) Cambridge: Harvard University, 1917.

MERCER, HENRY C. *The Hill Caves of Yucatán.* Philadelphia, 1896.

Mexican and Central American Antiquities, Calendar Systems and History. Twenty-four papers by Eduard Seler, E. Förstemann, Paul Schellhas, Carl Sapper, and E. P. Dieseldorff. Translated from the German under the supervision of Charles P. Bowditch. ("Bureau of American Ethnology, Smithsonian Institution," Bulletin 28.) Washington, D.C., 1904.

Mexico: Pre-Hispanic Paintings. (Volume X, UNESCO World Art Series). Greenwich, Connecticut: New York Graphic Society.

MITCHELL, JAMES LESLIE. *The Conquest of the Maya.* New York: E. P. Dutton and Company, Inc., 1935.

MORLEY, S. G. *The Ancient Maya.* 1st and 2nd editions. Stanford, California: Stanford University Press, 1946, 1947.

———. *The Ancient Maya.* 3rd edition. Revised by G. W. Brainerd. Stanford, California: Stanford University Press, 1956.

———. "The Historical Value of the Books of Chilam Balam," *American Journal of Archaeology,* 2nd ser., Vol. XV, No. 2 (1911).

———. *An Introduction to the Study of the Maya Hieroglyphs.* ("Bureau of American Ethnology, Smithsonian Institution," Bulletin 57.) Washington, D.C., 1915.

MORLEY, S. G. *Guide Book to the Ruins of Quiriguá.* Washington, D.C.: Carnegie Institution, 1935.

MORRIS, EARL H. *The Temple of the Warriors.* New York: Charles Scribner's Sons, 1931.

Popol Vuh: The Sacred Book of the Ancient Quiché Maya. Translated by Adrián Recinos. English version by Sylvanus G. Morley and Delia Goetz. Norman: University of Oklahoma Press, 1950.

PRESCOTT, WILLIAM H. *The Conquest of Mexico.* The Modern Library Edition. New York: Random House.

PROSKOURIAKOFF, T. *An Album of Maya Architecture.* ("Carnegie Institution of Washington Publication," No. 558.) Washington, D.C., 1946.

――――. "Mayapán, the Last Stronghold of a Civilization," *Scientific American,* May, 1955.

――――. *A Study of Classic Maya Sculpture.* ("Carnegie Institution of Washington Publication," No. 593.) Washington, D.C., 1950.

RECINOS, ADRIÁN, and GOETZ, DELIA. *The Annals of the Cakchiquels.* Norman: University of Oklahoma Press, 1953.

RICKETSON, O. G., JR., and RICKETSON, E. B. *Uaxactún, Guatemala, Group E, 1926-31.* Part I: The Excavations; Part II: The Artifacts. ("Carnegie Institution of Washington Publication," No. 477.) Washington, D.C., 1937.

RIVET, PAUL. Cités maya. Paris: A. Guillot, 1954.

ROYS, RALPH L. *The Book of Chilam Balam of Chumayel.* ("Carnegie Institution of Washington Publication," No. 438) Washington, D.C., 1933.

――――. *The Indian Background of Colonial Yucatán.* ("Carnegie Institution of Washington Publication," No. 548.) Washington, D.C., 1943.

RUPPERT, K., THOMPSON, J. E. S., and PROSKOURIAKOFF, T. *Bonampak, Chiapas, Mexico.* ("Carnegie Institution of Washington Publication," No. 602.) Washington, D.C., 1955.

RUZ LHUILLIER, ALBERTO. "Cámara secreta del Templo de las Inscripciones." *Tlatoani* (Mexico), Vol. I, Nos. 3-4 (1952).

Ruz Lhuillier, Alberto. "Estudio de la cripta del Templo de las Inscripciones en Palenque," *Tlatoani* (Mexico), Vol. I, Nos. 5-6 (1953).

————. "The Mystery of the Temple of the Inscriptions," *Archaeology,* Vol. VI, No. 1 (1953).

————. "La pirámide-tumba de Palenque." *Cuadernos Americanos* (Mexico), Vol. LXXIV (1954).

———— and Mason, J. A. "Mystery of the Mayan Temple." *The Saturday Evening Post,* August 29, 1953.

Sahagún, Fray Bernardino de. *A General History of the Things of New Spain,* Translated by Arthur J. O. Anderson and Charles E. Dibble. Santa Fe, New Mexico: School of American Research, 1957.

Satterthwaite, L. *Evolution of a Maya Temple.* ("University Museum Bulletin," Part I, Vol. 7, No. 4; Part II, Vol. 8, Nos. 2-3.) Philadelphia, 1939-40.

Séjourné, Laurette. *Palenque—Una Ciudad Maya.* Mexico: Fondo de Cultura Economica, 1952.

Shook, E. M. *The Temple of Kulkulcan at Mayapan.* ("Carnegie Institution of Washington, Current Reports," No. 20.) Washington, D.C., 1954.

Smith, A. Ledyard. *Archaeological Reconnaissance in Central Guatemala.* ("Carnegie Institution of Washington Publication," No. 608.) Washington, D.C., 1955.

Solís, J. F. Molina. *História de Yucatán.* Mérida, 1904.

Spence, Lewis. *The Gods of Mexico.* London, 1923.

Spinden, H. J. *Ancient Civilizations of Mexico and Central America.* ("American Museum of Natural History, Handbook Series," No. 3.) New York, 1917.

————. *Maya Art and Civilization.* Revised edition. Indian Hills, Colorado: The Falcon's Wing Press, 1957.

————. *The Origin and Distribution of Agriculture in America.* ("Proceedings International Congress Americanists, 19th Session, Washington, 1915.") Washington, D.C., 1917.

————. *The Reduction of Mayan Dates.* ("Papers of the Peabody Museum of American Archaeology and Ethnology," Vol. VI, No. 4.) Cambridge: Harvard University, 1924.

SPINDEN, H. J. *A Study of Maya Art*. ("Memoirs of the Peabody Museum of American Archaeology and Ethnology," Vol. VI.) Cambridge: Harvard University, 1913.

STEGGERDA, MORRIS. *Maya Indians of Yucatán*. ("Carnegie Institution of Washington Publication," No. 531.) Washington, D.C., 1941.

STEPHENS, JOHN L. *Incidents of Travel in Central America, Chiapas, and Yucatán*. Edited by Richard L. Predmore. New Brunswick, New Jersey: Rutgers University Press, 1949.

TEEPLE, J. E. *Maya Astronomy*. (*Contributions to American Archaeology*, Vol. I, No. 2. "Carnegie Institution of Washington Publication," No. 403.) Washington, D.C., 1931.

THOMPSON, E. H. *People of the Serpent*. Boston: Houghton Mifflin Company, 1932.

THOMPSON, J. Eric S. *A Correlation of the Mayan and European Calendars*. ("Field Museum of Natural History Publication," No. 241, Anthropological Series, Vol. XVIII, No. 1.) Chicago, 1927.

————. *Maya Arithmetic*. (*Contributions to American Anthropology*, Vol. VII, No. 36. "Carnegie Institution of Washington Publication," No. 528.) Washington, D.C., 1942.

————. *Maya Chronology: The Correlation Question*. (*Contributions to American Archaeology*, Vol. III, No. 14. "Carnegie Institution of Washington Publication," No. 456.) Washington, D.C., 1935.

————. *The Rise and Fall of Maya Civilization*. Norman: University of Oklahoma Press, 1954.

TOSCANO, S. *Art precolombino de Mexico y de la América Central*. Mexico: Universidad Nacional Autónoma de México, 1944.

TOZZER, A. M. *A Comparative Study of the Maya and the Lacandónes*. New York, 1907.

VAILLANT, GEORGE C. *The Aztecs of Mexico. Origin, Rise and Fall of the Aztec Nation*. New York: Doubleday, Doran and Company, Inc., 1941.

VILLAGRA CALETI, AGUSTÍN. *Bonampak, La Ciudad de los Muros Pintados*. Mexico: Instituto Nacional de Antropologia e Historia, 1940.

VON HAGEN, VICTOR WOLFGANG. *Maya Explorer*. Norman: University of Oklahoma Press, 1947.

Von Hagen, Victor Wolfgang. *Frederick Catherwood, Arch.* New York: Oxford University Press, 1950.

Willey, Gordon R. "The Structure of Ancient Maya Society: Evidence from the Southern Lowland," *American Anthropologist,* Vol. 58, No. 5 (1956).

——, Bullard, W. R., and Glass, J. B. "The Maya Community of Prehistoric Times," *Archaeology,* Vol. VIII, No. 1 (1955).

Wormington, H. M. *Ancient Man in North America.* Denver, Colorado: The Denver Museum of Natural History, 1957.

Index

Archaeological Sites in the Maya Area
SITES
GULF OF MEXICO
YUCATAN
T'HO
MAYAPÁN
UXMAL
KABAH
LABN
SAYIL
SANTA ROS
ETZNÁ
CHICHÉN ITZÁ
TULUM
QUINTANA ROO
CAMPECHE
RÍO BEC
EL PALMAR
CALAKMUL
JONUTA
TABASCO
NDURAS